ReviseandShine

KS2Science

Simon Greaves and Anne Loadman

INTRODUCTION

In the weeks leading up to the National Tests, your child will be given practice tests and revision at school. However, many children benefit from doing extra revision at home. This book will help your child prepare for their National Test in Science through a carefully planned eight–week revision period.

The book is divided into eight revision units. Each unit covers a whole week's work and for every day within that week there are two pages of content. The first page presents all the information your child needs to know in an interesting and friendly way, and the second page (the practice page) assesses their understanding of that information. The final part of the book contains a practice test (see page 85), following the format of the National Maths Test, as well as a comprehensive answer section (see page 94). Guidance is also given on how to award a level (see page 96).

Successful revision

The key to using this book successfully is to know the ability of your child. Although the book has been designed to fit an eight–week plan, it could just as successfully be spread over a longer time. However, covering the book in a shorter time is not advised, as each child needs time to develop the depth of knowledge required. You can use the checklist on page 4 to monitor progress and give your child a sense of achievement.

Be guided by the ability of your child and don't be tempted to rush. If you have covered a topic and they still seem unsure, move on but come back to the other topic later. Sometimes children need time to assimilate knowledge and understanding and what seemed impossible on one day, will seem easier on another. Always try to build on success.

Talk to your child about the content of the information pages, to make sure they are clear about all the terms before they attempt the practice pages. Clear up uncertainties as you go along.

Revision tips

- Regular and frequent revision is most effective.
- Don't try and cover too much at once.
- Focus on one topic at a time and go at your child's pace.
- Try not to feel frustrated if your child can't do or remember something.
- Reinforce correct answers by repeating the correct answer back to your child to show how they should be answering a particular question.
- Give hints and praise effort.

What are the National Tests?

The National Tests take place in May each year. The tests for KS2 are in English, Mathematics and Science and are administered over the course of a week. The National Test in Science at Key Stage 2 is made up of two papers, Test A and Test B, each with a time allowance of 45 minutes. Each paper has a total of 40 marks, giving a final test score out of 80. Children are required to answer different types of question covering most, if not all, of the programme of study for Key Stage 2 Science in the following three areas:

- knowledge and understanding of scientific facts
- knowledge and understanding of scientific concepts
- knowledge and understanding of the skills involved in scientific enquiry.

This latter category is the newest focus of the test, checking on children's ability to apply their knowledge and understanding by drawing conclusions, describing what is being investigated and identifying variables. For this reason, a number of this newer type of question have been included in the practice test in this book.

The tests are marked by external examiners and the scripts are returned to the school at the beginning of July. The marks for each paper are totalled and a level is given, usually between 3 and 5. Level 4 is the average level to be achieved by an 11-year-old. It is important to note that the tests cannot be passed or failed. They measure the level at which your child is currently working.

CONTENTS

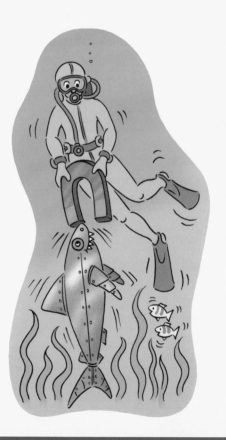

REVISION CHECKLIST

Scientific Enquiry	Page numbers	Revised
Planning an experiment	pages 5-6	
Carrying out an experiment	pages 7-8	
Shadow investigation	pages 13–14	
Magnetic forces investigation	pages 23-24	
Forces investigation	pages 33-34	
Plant growth investigation	pages 43-44	
Pulse rate investigation	pages 53-54	
Healthy eating investigation	pages 63-64	
Evaporation investigation	pages 73-74	
Soil investigation	pages 81-82	
Life Processes and Living Things		
Life processes	pages 35-36	
Keys and classification	pages 37-38	
Life cycle of a flowering plant	pages 39-40	
Plant growth	pages 41-42	
Habitats and adaptation	pages 45-46	
Food chains	pages 47-48	
Health	pages 49-50	
Heart and exercise	pages 51-52	
Teeth	pages 55-56	
Skeleton and muscles	pages 57-58	
Human life cycle	pages 59-60	
Micro-organisms	pages 61-62	
Materials and their Properties		
Properties of materials	pages 65-66	
Solids, liquids, gases	pages 67-68	
Reversible changes	pages 69-70	
Non-reversible changes	pages 71-72	
Methods of separation	pages 75-76	
Rocks and soils	pages 77-78	
Conductors and insulators	pages 79-80	
Physical Processes		
Light	pages 9-10	
Light and shadow	pages 11-12	
Earth, moon and sun	pages 15-16	
Sound	pages 17-18	
Electricity	pages 19-20	
Magnetic forces	pages 21-22	
Forces	pages 25-26	
Gravity	pages 27-28	
Upthrust	pages 29-30	
Friction and air resistance	pages 31-32	

PLANNING AN EXPERIMENT

What you need to know

1 Know that an investigation has a purpose.

2 Know that some factors in an experiment are kept the same whilst others are changed.

3 Know how to make sure an experiment is done fairly and safely.

THE PURPOSE

- **Investigation** is an essential part of science but you need to know what you want to find out, the **purpose**.
- You need to: **plan** the experiments, work out what you are going to **measure** and what **equipment** you will need.

THE FACTORS

- You need to think about which things you will change in each test and which must be kept the same.
- You need to list all the **factors** that might affect what you are investigating. These are sometimes called **variables** because they are things that can be changed or varied.

If you were investigating how plants grow you would need to consider: the soil they are planted in; the amount of light and heat; how often they are watered; how much water is used.

- You need to test one factor at a time so you can observe the effect of that particular factor.

FAIR TESTS

- It is very important that you carry out your tests fairly.
- Use the same equipment for each test.
- Measure things accurately using the same measuring equipment and take measurements at the same times.
- Make sure you don't do something in one test which you haven't done in the others.

SAFETY
- Always work safely. In some experiments you may need to use chemicals, hot liquids, burners or candles, glass beakers, heavy objects or scissors.
- Always use the equipment sensibly and use protective clothing if needed.
- Wash your hands and the equipment after you've used it.

Remember
Choosing the correct equipment is important, especially measuring equipment. It must be suitable for the type of experiment you are doing. (Bathroom scales are of no use if you need to measure a spoonful of salt because they would not be accurate enough.)

PLANNING AN EXPERIMENT

1 Look at the measuring equipment.

Which piece of equipment would you use to measure:

(a) the time it takes for a piece of paper to fall to the ground? ⬜ 1 mark

(b) the height of a seedling? ⬜ 1 mark

(c) the temperature of water in a beaker? ⬜ 1 mark

A
B
C
D
E 12:07
F
G
H
I
J

2 Karim has four identical glass beakers. He puts equal amounts of sugar into each one. Then he pours the same amount of water at different temperatures into each beaker. He times how long it takes for the lump of sugar to dissolve in each beaker.

(a) What is the purpose of Karim's investigation?

_____ 1 mark

(b) Here are the factors which feature in his experiment.
Put a tick next to the one factor which is being changed.

The amount of water in the beaker. ⬜   The temperature of the water. ⬜

The amount of sugar. ⬜   The size of the beaker. ⬜ 1 mark

(c) Would it matter if Karim stirred the water in one of the beakers during the experiment? Explain your answer.

_____

_____ 1 mark

(d) Karim should take steps to make sure he carries out the experiment safely.
Give **TWO** things he needs to take care with in this experiment.

_____ 1 mark

_____ 1 mark

TOTAL ⬜

How did you score?

4 or less – try again!
5 or 6 – nearly there!
7 or 8 – well done!

6

CARRYING OUT AN EXPERIMENT

What you need to know

1 Know that the results of an experiment must be collected accurately, fairly and safely.

2 Know how to present results in tables, graphs and charts.

3 Know how to use results to make conclusions and explain outcomes.

ACCURACY AND FAIRNESS

- Read scales on equipment such as weighing scales, jugs, rulers, force meters and thermometers carefully.
- If possible, take the measurement more than once. If you are measuring how something is changing over time, make sure you measure it at regular intervals.
- Sometimes an experiment is repeated to make sure of the **results**.
- Always check your results for obvious mistakes.

PRESENTING RESULTS

- Record your results in a logical way. The usual way is to use a **table**.
- Sometimes a **chart** or **graph** will show your results more clearly.

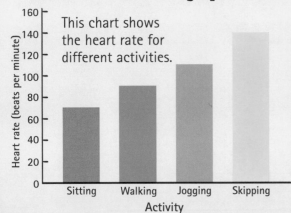

This chart shows the heart rate for different activities.

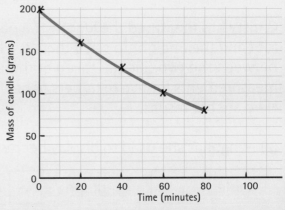

This line graph shows that the longer a candle burns, the less it weighs.

CONCLUSIONS AND OUTCOMES

- The next step is to make a conclusion: a statement about the things you have been investigating.
- Finally, see if you can explain your outcomes (results).

In the bar chart above, you would expect the heart rate to increase with stronger exercise, as the heart needs to get oxygen to the muscles more quickly.

- Sometimes you can also use your results to predict others.

By extending the line graph above, you could predict that after two hours the candle would have a mass of about 50 g.

CARRYING OUT AN EXPERIMENT

1 Jade has been carrying out an investigation to find out which habitat woodlice prefer. She counted the number of woodlice she found in different places around the garden.
Here are her results.

Habitat	Number of woodlice
under a stone	12
under a pile of dry leaves	1
in a damp corner of a shed	10
in a pile of sand	0
under a bush	4

(a) Complete the bar chart using Jade's results.

2 marks

(b) Jade carried out the same experiment the next day.
Why did she do this?

_____

1 mark

(c) What conclusion could she make about the type of habitats woodlice prefer?

_____

2 marks

2 Christy has measured the length of a person's foot and their height to see if there is a link between the two. She has taken both these measurements for five members of her family. Here are her results.

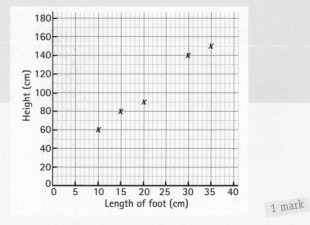

(a) What has she used to display her results?

table ☐   graph ☐

pie chart ☐   diagram ☐

1 mark

(b) Her cousin is 100 cm tall and her foot length is 25 cm.
Add this point to the other results above.

1 mark

(c) What do you think Christy's results tell her?

Taller people have smaller feet. ☐   Short people are smaller. ☐

Taller people have larger feet. ☐   Some people have large feet. ☐

1 mark

TOTAL ☐

LIGHT

What you need to know

1 Know that light travels from its source in a straight line.

2 Know that we see light sources because the light enters our eyes.

3 Know that light is reflected from surfaces.

4 Know that some materials allow different amounts of light to pass through them.

TRAVELLING LIGHT

- **Sources** of light include:

  light bulbs   lighted candles   torches   the sun   stars

- Light travels in **straight lines** from the source of light and bounces off objects.
- We can see light sources and objects because the light from them travels to, and enters, our eyes.

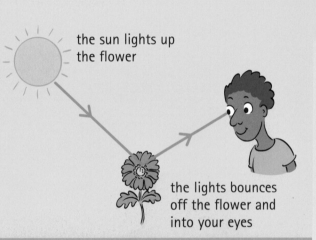

the sun lights up the flower

the lights bounces off the flower and into your eyes

Mirror info

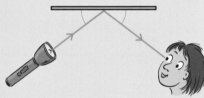

Light bounces off a mirror at the same angle as it hits it.

Car drivers use mirrors to help them see objects behind them.

REFLECTED LIGHT

- On a cloudy night in the middle of the countryside where there are no street lights it is very, very dark. You cannot see objects because there is no light to **reflect** off them.
- In towns and cities it is never completely dark because there is still light coming from some sources.

  Shiny objects, such as **mirrors** and metal, reflect light well
  Dark, dull objects do not reflect light well

LIGHT AND MATERIALS

- Light cannot travel through **opaque** materials.
- **Transparent** materials allow light to pass through them completely.
- **Translucent** materials allow some light to pass through them.

MATERIALS
Opaque   - brick, wood, cardboard
Transparent - glass, polythene
Translucent - tissue paper, some thin fabrics

LIGHT

1 (a) Zoe is investigating whether some objects let light pass through them.
She is using a torch as her light source.

Tick **THREE** other light sources.

a mirror ☐   a lighted candle ☐   a switched-on TV set ☐

the sun ☐   the earth ☐   a window ☐

3 marks

(b) Zoe shines the torch on some objects.
Draw a line from each object to the correct word.

coloured tissue paper

clear glass bottle

piece of wood

pair of nylon tights

transparent

translucent

opaque

2 marks

(c) Zoe then shines the torch on to a mirror.
Draw lines, with arrows, to show how the light
travels from the torch to her eye.

2 marks

(d) Zoe's father wears glasses. The lenses become darker when he is outside
on a sunny day. Give a reason why the glasses are designed to do this.

_____

1 mark

_____

TOTAL ☐

How did
you score?

4 or less – try again!
5 or 6 – nearly there!
7 or 8 – well done!

LIGHT AND SHADOW

What you need to know

1 Understand how a shadow is formed.

2 Know that the position of the sun in the sky can shorten or lengthen shadows.

SHADOWS

• When an object blocks out the light, a **shadow** is formed.

If light is blocked by an object made from an **opaque** material, a black shadow is formed.

Translucent objects form faint shadows.

• An object made from a **transparent** material, such as a window, does not form a shadow.

THE SUN AND SHADOWS

• The sun is our main light source and casts shadows.
• The sun appears to move across the sky during the day although it is actually the earth that moves.
• The sun affects the length of shadows during the day.
• Shadows are shortest at midday and longest at the beginning and end of the day.

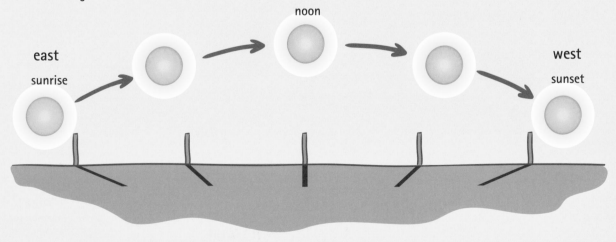

LIGHT AND SHADOW

1 (a) Lee notices that the sun is in a different position in the sky at different times of the day. What causes these changes?

_____

1 mark

(b) Look at the diagrams below.

9:00 a.m.	11:00 a.m.	noon	2:00 p.m.

(i) What happens to the shadow as the sun appears to move across the sky?

_____

1 mark

(ii) At what time of day is a shadow at its shortest?

[   ]

1 mark

(c) Sketch the position of the sun and what the shadow would look like at 4:00 p.m.

1 mark

2 Simon shines a light on some objects which have a piece of white board behind them.

Tick the objects that you think will form a dark shadow.

a clear plastic bottle [   ]   an empty jam jar [   ]   a comb [   ]

the lens of a magnifying glass [   ]   a wooden ruler [   ]

2 marks

3 Look at the door and its shadow.

There are **TWO** things wrong with the way the shadow has been drawn.
What are they?

(i) _____   1 mark

(ii) _____   1 mark

TOTAL [   ]

SHADOW INVESTIGATION

An object made from opaque material will cast a dark shadow when a light is shone onto it.

Investigate how the shadow changes depending on how close it is to the light source.

You will need
a torch
a small object, such as an ornament or container
(remember it must be opaque)
a large piece of white paper
some tape
a ruler or tape measure
a pencil

What to do

1   Set up the equipment as shown in the diagram.

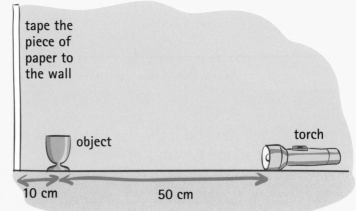

tape the piece of paper to the wall

object

torch

10 cm   50 cm

2   Darken the room so that you can see the shadow of the object better.

3   Draw around the shadow on the paper with a pencil. Label this outline '1'.

4   Now move the object 10 cm further towards the torch. Draw around the shadow on the same piece of paper and label this outline '2'.

5   Keep doing this until the object is next to the torch.

6   Measure the height of the outline of each shadow and record your measurements on the table below.

Test number	Distance of object from torch (cm)	Height of shadow (cm)
1	50	
2	40	
3	30	
4	20	
5	10	
6	0	

Now answer the questions on page 14.

1 Plot your results on the graph below.

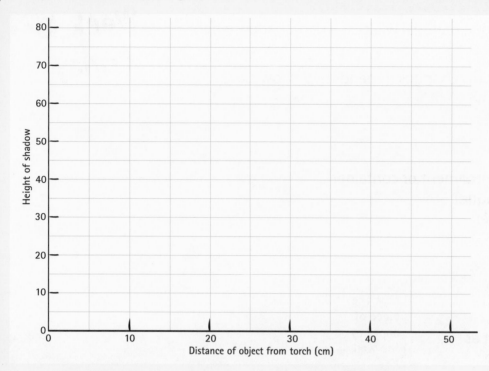

2 What do your results tell you about the size of an object's shadow and its distance from the light source?

_____

_____

_____

_____

3 Did you notice anything else about the shadow as the object got closer to the light source?

_____

_____

_____

_____

EARTH, MOON AND SUN

What you need to know

1 Know that the shapes of the sun, moon and earth are spheres.

2 Know the orbits of the earth and moon.

3 Understand how night and day occur.

4 Know that the position of the sun is fixed and that the earth moves around it.

Sphere shaped
The sun, moon and earth are all spheres in shape, although not perfect ones.

ORBIT FACTS

- The path in which a planet or moon travels is called an **orbit**. 'Orbits' is the proper word for 'travels around' when talking about planets and moons.
- It takes **365 days** for the earth to orbit the sun.
- The earth is kept in its orbit by the **gravitational pull** of the sun.
- The moon orbits the earth once every **28 days**.
- We get a different view of the moon each night because we only see the part of the moon which is lit up by the sun.

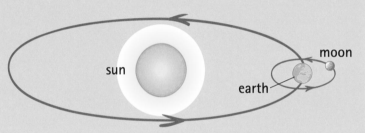

The orbits of the moon and earth.

NIGHT AND DAY

- As the earth orbits the sun it **rotates** on its **tilted axis** causing day and night.

- The part of the earth on which the sun is shining is experiencing day whilst the other side of the earth, which is in darkness, is experiencing night.

Did you know?
- The sun is in a fixed position and it is the earth that travels around it.
- Apart from the earth and the moon, there are eight planets which travel around the sun as well. These are Mercury, Venus, Mars, Jupiter, Saturn, Uranus, Neptune and Pluto.

EARTH, MOON AND SUN

1 Which one of these statements is true?

The sun orbits the earth. ☐   The sun orbits the moon. ☐

The earth orbits the sun. ☐   The moon orbits the sun. ☐   *1 mark*

2 What type of force keeps a planet or moon in its orbit?

friction ☐   weight ☐   gravity ☐   upthrust ☐   *1 mark*

3 Which word best describes the shape of the moon?

circle ☐   sphere ☐   oval ☐   cylinder ☐   *1 mark*

4 Melissa looks out of her window at the moon. It is shining brightly in the sky.

(a) Where does the light come from which makes the moon shine?

_____   *1 mark*

(b) Melissa draws a diagram of the moon she sees.

After a few nights she draws another
diagram of what the moon looks like now.

Explain why the moon looks different on different nights.

_____

_____   *2 marks*

(c) Melissa decides to record what the moon looks like every night for the
next two weeks. Why might this not always be possible?

_____   *1 mark*

5 How long does it take the moon to orbit the earth?

365 days ☐   100 days ☐   28 days ☐   7 days ☐   *1 mark*

TOTAL ☐

SOUND

What you need to know

1 Know that sound is made when objects vibrate.

2 Understand the difference between pitch and loudness.

3 Understand that the pitch and loudness of some vibrating objects may be changed.

4 Know that vibrations from sound sources can travel through different materials.

VIBRATIONS

- All **sound** is caused by **vibration**. You cannot always see the vibration but it must be there to cause a sound.
- Sounds can come from different **sources**, for example, your voice, a guitar, the TV, a tuning fork or a car engine.
- No noise occurs when a sound source stops vibrating.

PITCH AND LOUDNESS

- **Pitch** is a measure of how high or low a sound is.
- The pitch of a sound is affected by the size and shape of the sound source.

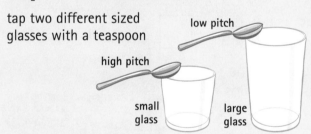

tap two different sized glasses with a teaspoon

low pitch

high pitch

small glass

large glass

low pitch
longer length of ruler

'twang' a ruler on the edge of a table

high pitch

shorter length of ruler

- **Loudness** is a measure of how loud or soft a sound is.
- Loudness can be varied by how hard you hit, blow, pluck or shake the sound source. The harder you hit, the louder the sound.

blow gently to get a quiet sound

blow hard to get a loud sound

TRAVELLING SOUND

- We hear sounds when vibrations from a sound source reach our ears.
- Sound can travel through different materials such as air, water, glass, stone, wood or metal. It travels better through some materials than others.
- Sound cannot travel through a **vacuum** (a space with no air in it).

SOUND

1 Faye has poured some water into bottles.

A   B   C   D   E   F

(a) If Faye taps each one gently with a pencil which bottle would make:

the lowest-pitched sound? ☐   the highest-pitched sound? ☐

2 marks

(b) What could Faye do to make each sound louder?

_____

1 mark

2 Gary hits a cymbal and lets it vibrate. It makes a very loud sound.

(a) What would the sound be like after 5 seconds?

Louder than when it was first hit. ☐   Silent. ☐

Quieter than when. it was first hit. ☐   As loud as it was when it was first hit. ☐

1 mark

(b) What would the sound be like after 5 minutes?

Louder than when it was first hit. ☐   Silent. ☐

Quieter than when it was first hit. ☐   As loud as it was when it was first hit. ☐

1 mark

(c) Gary hits the cymbal again. He then nips the edge of the cymbal between his thumb and finger. The sound stops. Explain why the sound stops.

_____

1 mark

(d) Gary puts some ear plugs into his ears and hits the cymbal again. The sound he hears is much quieter. Explain why the sound is quieter.

_____ *1 mark*

ear defenders

3 Sally notices a workman digging up the road with a drill. He is wearing ear defenders over his ears.

Why do you think it is important that he wears them?

_____

_____

1 mark

TOTAL ☐

How did you score?

4 or less – try again!
5 or 6 – nearly there!
7 or 8 – well done!

ELECTRICITY

What you need to know

1 Know that electricity can be supplied from the mains and from batteries.

2 Understand how switches can be used to break a circuit.

3 Know the factors that make a bulb brighter in a circuit.

4 Know the symbols for items used in simple electrical circuits.

CIRCUITS

- All electrical devices use **circuits**.
- A circuit needs a power source, such as a battery, wires and other devices such as **switches**, **motors**, **buzzers** and **bulbs**. If the wires are correctly connected to a battery, electricity will be able to flow through it.
- Electricity can only flow in one direction.

> **Sources of electricty**
> Some electrical devices use electricity from the **mains**, e.g. cookers, hairdryers or lights. Other smaller electrical devices use electricity from **batteries** (or **cells**), e.g. calculators, torches or mobile phones.

Here is a simple circuit.

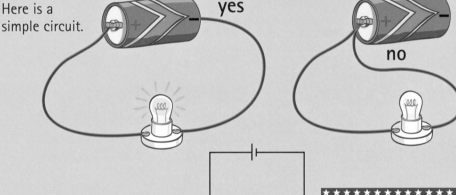

This is the circuit diagram for the circuit marked 'yes' above.

- A switch can be added to a circuit to allow the flow of electricity to be broken.

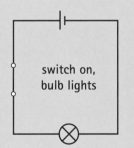
switch on, bulb lights

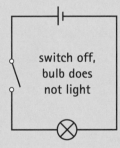
switch off, bulb does not light

- Adding more batteries to the circuit or shortening the wires in it will make the bulb shine brighter.

Remember
Circuits are usually drawn as diagrams using these symbols.

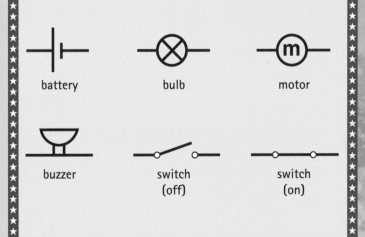

battery   bulb   motor

buzzer   switch (off)   switch (on)

ELECTRICITY

1 Look at the picture of the circuit.

(a) Why will the buzzer not work in this circuit?

_____

(b) In the box draw a diagram of a circuit that will make the buzzer work. Use the symbols below.

battery

buzzer

switch (on)

(c) The sound made by the buzzer in this circuit is very quiet. What could be added to the circuit to make the buzzer sound louder?

(d) The buzzer is replaced by a bulb. The switch is closed so that electricity flows through the bulb. Write down **TWO** things that will happen to the bulb.

(i) _____

(ii) _____

2 In very bad weather the mains electricity supply can be broken. This means that lots of electrical devices in the home stop working or cannot be used.

(a) Write down **TWO** devices which would be affected in this way.

(i) _____ (ii) _____

(b) Sammy has a digital alarm clock which uses mains electricity. He notices that during a break in the electricity supply his digital alarm clock is still working. Explain how this might be possible.

_____

TOTAL

How did you score?

4 or less – try again!
5 or 6 – nearly there!
7 or 8 – well done!

MAGNETIC FORCES

What you need to know

1 Know that magnets exert forces on each other.

2 Know which materials are magnetic.

3 Know that magnets exert forces on objects made from magnetic materials.

MAGNETS

- Magnets exert **forces** on each other. These forces are strongest at their **poles**.
- **Magnets** have two poles: north and south.
- If you try to put two magnets together with the same poles touching, for example north and north, the magnets will **repel**, or push away from, each other.
- If you try to put two magnets together with different poles touching, for example, north and south, they will **attract**, or move towards, each other.

MAGNETIC MATERIALS

- Some materials have **magnetic** properties: they are attracted to magnets.
- Iron and steel are magnetic.
  Most other metals, such as copper and aluminium, are **non-magnetic**.
- Other materials, such as plastic, rubber, wood, paper and glass, are non-magnetic.

MAGNETIC FORCES

- Some magnets are stronger than others.

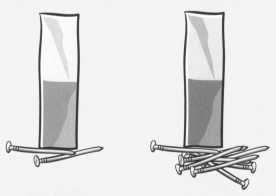

If each magnet is dipped into a dish of steel pins the stronger magnet will pick up more pins than the weaker magnet.

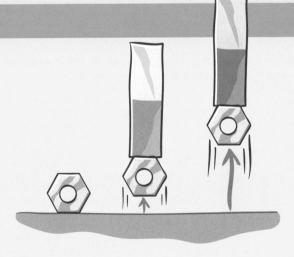

A stronger magnet will pick up a steel nut from further away than a weaker magnet.

MAGNETIC FORCES

Object	Magnetic or non-magnetic
wooden peg	x
iron nail	
steel paperclip	
aluminium foil	
plastic spoon	

1 Some objects are made from materials which have magnetic properties.

Put a tick next to each object which is magnetic.
Put a cross if it is non-magnetic.

2 marks

2 Stephanie is investigating magnets.
She has two identical bar magnets.
She puts them near each other in two different positions.

N S   N S   ☐

N S   S N   ☐

What do you think will happen?
Write ATTRACT or REPEL in the box.

2 marks

3 Ellie has four magnets which are the same size but different strengths.
One at a time, she holds each one just above a dish of steel pins.
She knows that the pins are made of magnetic material so they will be attracted to the magnet. For each magnet Ellie counts the number of pins picked up by it.

(a) What is the purpose of Ellie's investigation?

To find out if a magnet is magnetic. ☐

To compare the strength of different magnets. ☐

To find out if steel pins are magnetic. ☐

To find out how many pins a magnet can pick up. ☐

1 mark

(b) She records her results in a bar chart.

How many pins does magnet B pick up? ☐

1 mark

(c) Which is the strongest magnet? ☐

1 mark

4 Some cupboard doors have magnetic catches.

Suggest a reason for using these on cupboard doors.

_____

_____

1 mark

TOTAL ☐

MAGNETIC FORCE INVESTIGATION

A magnet can attract objects which are made from magnetic materials, such as iron and steel. Magnets can exert different-sized magnetic forces.

Investigate the strength of the magnetic force exerted by a magnet.

You will need
a bar magnet
steel pins (or paperclips, safety pins, staples)
different materials such as paper, thick card, aluminium foil, fabric

What to do

1   Spread out the pins on a flat surface.

2   Hold one end of the bar magnet just above the pins.

3   Move the magnet away and then count the number of pins the magnet has picked up.

4   Put these pins back with the others and repeat.

5   Record both results in the table below.

Material	Number of pins picked up	
	1st attempt	2nd attempt
none		
paper		

6   Now wrap the end of the magnet with paper.

7   Repeat the experiment twice as before.

8   Use the table to record the number of pins picked up.

9   Repeat this experiment for different materials.

Now answer the questions on page 24.

1 Why is it important to obtain two sets of results for each material?

_____

_____

_____

2 What does the number of pins picked up suggest about the strength of the magnetic force exerted by the magnet?

_____

_____

_____

3 How was the strength of the magnet affected by each material? Write a sentence about the effect on each material.

_____

_____

_____

4 Does a magnet still work under water? Use the box below to plan your own experiment then carry it out.

FORCES

What you need to know

1 Know that forces are pushes and pulls acting in a particular direction.

2 Represent forces using arrows in diagrams.

3 Understand the effects on an object of balanced or unbalanced forces.

DIRECTION AND *SIZE* OF FORCES

- Arrows are used in diagrams to show the **directions** and **sizes** of forces.

  The size of the arrow shows the size of the force. The direction of the arrow shows the direction in which the force is acting.

BALANCED FORCES

Remember
Forces are measured in Newtons (N).

- When two forces are **balanced**, the arrows are of an **equal** size and point in opposite directions.

Push the palms of your hands together. The force **exerted** by your left hand is completely balanced by the force from your right hand.

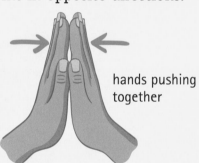

hands pushing together

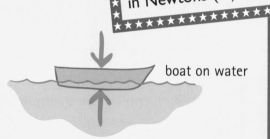

boat on water

The downwards force exerted by a boat on the water is completely balanced by the upwards force exerted by the water on the boat.

- When forces acting on an object are balanced, the object stays still: the two hands stay together in the same place and the boat stays on the surface of the water.

UNBALANCED FORCES

- **Unbalanced** forces can make things move, speed up, slow down or change direction.

If the left hand pushes harder than the right hand, both hands move to the right, in the direction of the bigger force.

pushing to right

load in boat causing it to sink

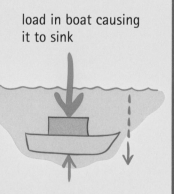

If a very heavy load is put into the boat, it will start to sink downwards because the downwards force is larger than the upwards force from the water.

FORCES

1 The pictures below show situations where the forces are balanced.

Use arrows to show the direction and size of the forces acting on these objects.   *3 marks*

2 Here is a ball at rest. It is about to be kicked by the boy's foot.

Describe what will happen to the ball when it is kicked and after it has been kicked. Try to use the words 'force', 'balanced' and 'unbalanced' in your answer.

_____

_____   *2 marks*

3 Callum is going on a hot air balloon trip. While the balloon is on the ground the upthrust from the hot air inside the balloon is balanced by the weight of the balloon and basket.

(a) When they are ready to set off, the person controlling the balloon throws some weights out of the basket. What will happen now?

_____   *1 mark*

(b) Draw arrows to show the size and direction of the forces acting on the balloon now.   *1 mark*

(c) At the end of the trip the balloon needs to be brought back down to the ground. Which force must be changed? Explain your answer.

_____

_____   *1 mark*

TOTAL [   ]

GRAVITY

What you need to know

1. Know that all objects exert a force due to gravity.

2. Understand the difference between weight and mass.

DOWNWARD PULL

- **Gravity** is the **downward** pull of the earth towards its centre.
- All objects on the earth, no matter where they are, feel a force due to the earth's gravity.

What happens when you jump up in the air?
No matter how hard you jump you will always come back down due to the pull of gravity.
If gravity was less, you would be able to jump higher.
If it was greater, your body would feel heavier and you would not be able to jump as high.

WEIGHT OR *MASS*?

- **Weight** is actually a force. It is the force caused by gravity on an object.

- The **mass** of an object is measured in kilograms (kg) but its weight is measured in **Newtons** (N).

- Weight is measured using a forcemeter. There is a spring inside it which stretches in proportion to the weight of an object pulling down on it. The bigger the weight, the more the spring stretches.

1 N

A forcemeter measuring the weight of an apple.

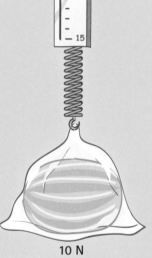

10 N

A forcemeter measuring the weight of a watermelon.

Work out your weight in Newtons
First find your mass in kilograms using a set of bathroom scales. Multiply your mass by 10. This will give you your approximate weight in Newtons.

weight = 38 x 10 = 380 N

Did you know?
Gravity exists on the moon as well as on the earth but it is not as strong as on the earth.

GRAVITY

1 A cat walking along a windowsill knocks over a plant pot. What is the name of the force that makes the plant pot fall to the ground?

1 mark

2 Jack has been using a forcemeter to measure the force due to the gravity of different objects. For each object, he recorded the force reading and measured the length of the spring in the forcemeter.

Object	Length of spring (centimetres)	Weight (Newtons)
book	3	6
pineapple	5	10
jug	3·5	7
toy car	1	2
video tape	4	4

(a) Which object produced the most force?

1 mark

(b) There is a mistake in his results for one of the objects. Which object has incorrect results?

1 mark

(c) How do you know this? _____

_____

1 mark

(d) What should Jack do to check that he has not made any other mistakes?

_____

1 mark

(e) Describe what Jack's results tell him about the force due to the gravity of each object and the length of the spring in the forcemeter.

_____

1 mark

(f) Jack now measures the force produced by a bunch of keys. The reading on the forcemeter is 4 Newtons. What would be the length of the spring?

cm

1 mark

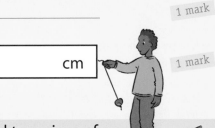

3 Paul is standing on a sloping path. He is holding a conker tied to a piece of string. What is wrong with this picture? Explain your answer.

_____

_____

1 mark

TOTAL

UPTHRUST

What you need to know

1 Know that water exerts a force called upthrust on an object in it.

2 Understand the relationship between upthrust and gravity.

UPWARD PUSH

- **Upthrust** is the upward push on an object in water.
- If the upthrust on an object is equal to the downwards force from **gravity** then an object will **float**.
- If an extra downwards force is exerted on the object, the forces are no longer **balanced** and the object goes under the water.

The ball floats as the forces are balanced.

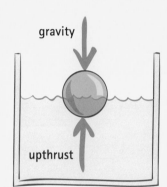

gravity

upthrust

Gravity and the force of the hand push the ball under the water.

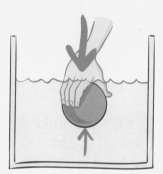

UPTHRUST AND GRAVITY

- If the force of an object due to gravity is greater than the upthrust from the water, the object will **sink**.

When the pebble is placed on the surface of the water it sinks to the bottom. The forces are unbalanced.

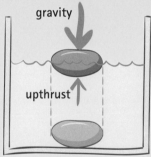

gravity

upthrust

- If an object is weighed in water, it will weigh less than in air. This is because the upthrust cancels out some of the object's weight.

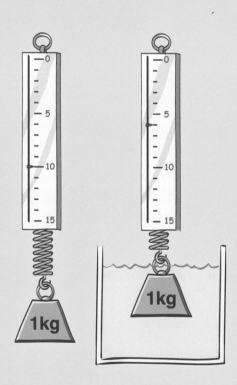

UPTHRUST

1 The forcemeter (opposite) can be used to measure the weights of objects. The forcemeter is made up of a spring, a measuring scale and a hook.

(a) What causes an object to have weight?

_____ 1 mark

(b) Claire attaches a stone to the hook on the forcemeter and uses it to measure the weight of a stone in air.

What is the weight of the stone in air?

| Newtons | 1 mark

(c) Claire then weighed the same stone in water.
Its weight in water was 10 Newtons.
What happens to the length of the spring in the forcemeter when the stone is placed in the water?

_____
_____ 1 mark

(d) Why does the stone weigh less in water than it does in air?

_____
_____ 1 mark

2 A rubber ball is placed on the surface of the water in a tank. It floats.

(a) Draw arrows to show the forces acting on the ball.

2 marks

(b) The ball is taken out and a pebble placed on the surface of the water.
It sinks. What causes the pebble to sink?

_____
_____ 2 marks

TOTAL | |

How did you score?

4 or less – try again!
5 or 6 – nearly there!
7 or 8 – well done!

FRICTION AND AIR RESISTANCE

What you need to know

1 Understand what is meant by friction and air resistance and recognize situations where they happen.

2 Know that friction produces heat.

FRICTION

- **Friction** is a force that tries to stop things sliding against each other.
- Friction can be a useful force.

It gives us **grip** between our shoes and the path when we walk. It gives grip between the tyres on a car and the road when steering and turning.

force driving the car

friction

When a car breaks, it slows down because the force driving it is smaller than the friction forces between the tyres and the road.

- There are times when we want to reduce friction, for example, when sledging or ice skating.

Friction can be reduced by making the amount of one surface touching another smaller, for example, sledges have thin runners. Friction can also be reduced by polishing, or oiling, surfaces to lessen the grip between them. The smoother the surface the less friction there is.

FRICTION AND HEAT

- Friction produces **heat**.

If you rub your hands together gently they become warm. If you do it harder, they get hotter.

AIR RESISTANCE

- There is friction between the air and objects moving in it. It is called **air resistance** and it slows down objects moving through it. The size and shape of the object affects the size of the force of air resistance.

The streamlined shape of the sports car allows air to pass more easily over it and this reduces the air resistance.

The parachute canopy needs to create a large air resistance force to slow it down.

FRICTION AND AIR RESISTANCE

1 Yusef is taking part in a cycle race. He wears a specially shaped helmet.

(a) Which force is he trying to reduce?

gravity ☐   air resistance ☐   upthrust ☐   weight ☐

1 mark

(b) Why would he want to reduce this force?

_____

1 mark

(c) Which force is acting between the tyres on his cycle and the road?

magnetic force ☐   gravity ☐   upthrust ☐   friction ☐

1 mark

(d) Yusef uses his brakes to slow down. What effect will this have on the force acting between his tyres and the road?

_____

1 mark

2 Kim and Bryony are testing how long it takes for objects to fall to the ground.
Bryony thinks that they should use this clock to time how long it takes for each object to fall.

(a) Why would this clock not be suitable?

_____

1 mark

(b) Bryony drops a pebble, a potato and a cricket ball, one at a time, from an upstairs window. Kim times how long it takes for each to fall to the ground. Which do you think will take the least time to fall?

The pebble will take least time. ☐   The cricket ball will take least time. ☐

The potato will take least time. ☐   They will all take the same time. ☐

1 mark

(c) Bryony then drops a piece of thin card, a paper tissue and a bead, one at a time, from the window. All three objects have the same weight. The times taken for each to fall to the ground are shown opposite.

Object	Time (seconds)
bead	1·0
thin card	4·3
paper tissue	6·8

Explain why it takes a different time for each object to fall to the ground.

_____

2 marks

TOTAL ☐

FORCES INVESTIGATION

If a single force is exerted on an object in a certain direction the object will move in the same direction. The size of the force will affect how far the object moves.

Investigate exerting different-sized forces on an object.

You will need
a small piece of card
a long elastic band
two nails hammered into a short plank of wood
(ask an adult to do this for you)
a ruler
a tape measure
a pencil

pull back to fire

measure how far the card travels forwards

What to do

1. Use the ruler to mark off a scale in centimetres along one side of the plank of wood, starting from where the nails are.

2. Loop the elastic band around the two nails to make a catapult.

3. Fold the small piece of card into a V shape.

4. Place the card V into the catapult, pull the elastic band back to a very short distance, say 1 cm or 2 cm (this will depend on how long your elastic band is and how far apart the nails are).

5. Let go.

6. Use the tape measure to measure how far the piece of card travels.

7. Record your results in the table.

8. Do this a few more times, each time pulling the elastic band further back.

Distance elastic band is pulled back (cm)	Distance travelled by V-shaped piece of card (cm)

Now answer the questions on page 34.

1 What can you say about the distance travelled by the card compared to the amount by which the elastic band is pulled back?

_____

_____

_____

2 What can you say about the amount of stretch in the elastic band and the force it gives to the piece of card?

_____

_____

_____

3 What can you say about the size of the force given to an object and the distance it travels?

_____

_____

_____

4 What surface did your piece of card travel along?

_____

5 What if you had carried out your experiment on a different surface? Would you have got the same results? Explain why.

_____

_____

_____

_____

LIFE PROCESSES

What you need to know

1 Know that there are several life processes common to all living things.

2 Know that there are some life processes common to many living things and some which are specific to certain living things.

COMMON PROCESSES

- All living things share the processes of:

reproduction (the process by which new living things are created), **nutrition** (feeding) and **growth**.

Reproduction
In green plants, pollen from the flowers fertilizes the egg in the adult plant to produce seeds. New plants grow from the seeds.
In animals and humans, eggs are fertilized, then start to grow and eventually produce a young animal or baby.
In humans and some animals, the egg is fertilized and grows inside the body.
Other animals lay eggs which develop outside the body, for example, birds and reptiles.

Nutrition
Nutrition is the process of taking in food.

Plants are able to make their own food in their leaves. Sunlight, water and carbon dioxide in the air are taken in by the plant and used to produce food and oxygen.

Animals and humans eat other animals and plants. Some animals eat only other animals, e.g. wolves, they are called carnivores. Some animals eat only plants, e.g. rabbits, they are called herbivores.

wolf   rabbit

Growth
This is the process by which a young living thing grows into an adult.

seed

Seeds grow into plants and keep growing bigger until they die.

seedling   plant

Young animals and babies grow into adult animals and humans and then stop growing at a certain age.

embryo   baby   adult

- There are three other life processes which both animals and plants have:

the ability to get rid of waste (excretion), respiration (breathing) and the ability to respond to changes around them (sensitivity).

SPECIFIC PROCESSES

- Animals have another life process: **movement**. Whilst parts of plants are able to move, for example, flowers turn towards the light, they cannot move from one place to another.
- Animals and humans are able to move around and move different parts of their body on their own.

LIFE PROCESSES

1 Tick the boxes below that apply to all living things.

swim ☐   grow ☐   fly ☐

reproduce ☐   lay eggs ☐   feed ☐

3 marks

2 Tick the boxes of the **THREE** living things listed below.

diamond ☐   cloud ☐

cat ☐   grass ☐

pebble ☐   mushroom ☐

3 marks

3 A plant is fixed in a pot and cannot move from that place.

(a) Give one way in which part of the plant is able to move.

_____

1 mark

(b) Name the process by which an adult plant produces a new plant.

_____

1 mark

TOTAL ☐

KEYS AND CLASSIFICATION

What you need to know

1 Know how familiar animals and plants can be identified using keys.

2 Know that different living things can have similar features or characteristics and that these may be grouped together.

USING KEYS

- A key can be used to identify an unknown living thing by studying its characteristics.

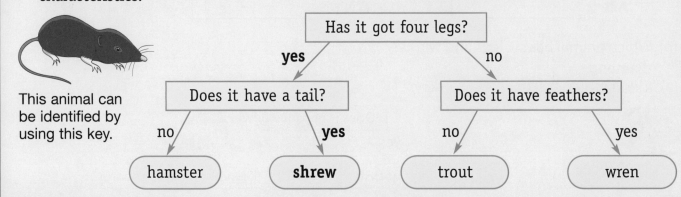

This animal can be identified by using this key.

Has it got four legs?

yes / no

Does it have a tail? / Does it have feathers?

no / **yes** / no / yes

hamster / **shrew** / trout / wren

GROUPING LIVING THINGS

- Animals and plants can be grouped together by the characteristics they have in common, such as a backbone, wings or flowers.
- Each group has a special name and particular characteristics.
- There are two main groups of animals: those that have a backbone (**vertebrates**) and those that do not (**invertebrates**).
- These can be further divided into smaller groups which have the same characteristics:

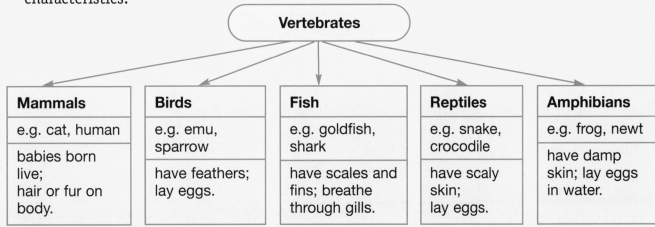

Vertebrates

Mammals	Birds	Fish	Reptiles	Amphibians
e.g. cat, human	e.g. emu, sparrow	e.g. goldfish, shark	e.g. snake, crocodile	e.g. frog, newt
babies born live; hair or fur on body.	have feathers; lay eggs.	have scales and fins; breathe through gills.	have scaly skin; lay eggs.	have damp skin; lay eggs in water.

Invertebrates include animals such as beetles, slugs, spiders, worms, earwigs and crabs.

Plants
There are two main groups of plants; those which flower and those which do not.

KEYS AND CLASSIFICATION

A

B

1 (a) Identify these animals using this key.

Has it got six legs?

yes → Has it got wings?

no → Has it got feathers?

Has it got wings?
- yes → bluebottle
- no → ant

Has it got feathers?
- no → salamander
- yes → sparrow

A is [   ]   **B** is [   ]   2 marks

(b) Which animal has six legs and wings? _____   1 mark

2 (a) Identify these plants using the key.

A

B

Does it produce flowers?

yes → Does it have thorns?

no → Does it produce spores?

Does it have thorns?
- yes → rose
- no → Are its seeds dispersed by wind?

Does it produce spores?
- yes → fern
- no → algae

Are its seeds dispersed by wind?
- yes → dandelion
- no → sweet pea

A is [   ]   **B** is [   ]   2 marks

(b) Does a fern produce flowers? _____   1 mark

3 Join the animals on the left to their correct classification group.

(Some of the groups may have more than one animal joined to them.)

frog   amphibians

polar bear
              reptiles
penguin

grass snake   birds

dolphin
              mammals   2 marks
owl

shark   fish

TOTAL [   ]

How did
you score?

4 or less – try again!
5 or 6 – nearly there!
7 or 8 – well done!

LIFE CYCLE OF A FLOWERING PLANT

What you need to know

1 Know the correct names for the parts of a flower.

2 Understand that reproduction involves pollination, producing seeds and dispersing them.

3 Describe the life cycle of a flowering plant.

FLOWER PARTS

- These are the main parts of a flower which are involved in the reproduction of the plant.

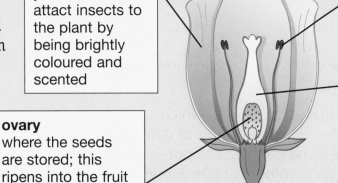

petals
attact insects to the plant by being brightly coloured and scented

ovary
where the seeds are stored; this ripens into the fruit

stamen
the male part of the plant which produces pollen

carpel
the female part of the plant, made up of the stigma, style and ovary

REPRODUCTION

- **Pollen** may be blown from one flower to another by the wind or carried to other flowers by visiting insects.
- Pollen sticks to the carpel where it fertilizes egg cells in the ovary to produce **seeds**.
- Seeds **disperse** in different ways, depending on the type of plant:

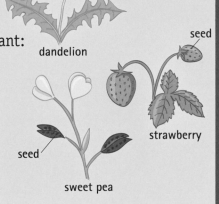

seed

dandelion

seed

strawberry

seed

sweet pea

wind	the wind blows some types of seed over long distances (e.g. dandelion)
animals	birds and animals eat the fruit of flowering plants and the undigested seeds pass through their systems (e.g. strawberry)
explosion	pods containing seeds explode and scatter the seeds (e.g. sweet pea).

PLANT LIFE CYCLE

This diagram shows the life cycle of a flowering plant.

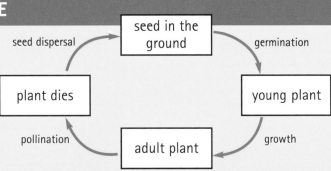

seed dispersal — seed in the ground — germination — young plant — growth — adult plant — pollination — plant dies

39

LIFE CYCLE OF A FLOWERING PLANT

1 Draw arrows from the boxes to the parts of the flower which do these jobs.

produces pollen

produces the fruit

supports the flower

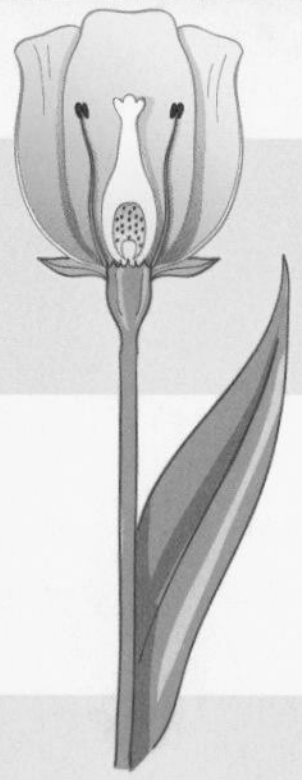

3 marks

2 When a bee lands on a flower some of the pollen sticks to its legs.

Explain why this is useful to the plant.

____

____ 1 mark

3 The petals on a flower are usually brightly coloured. This helps to attract insects to the flower.

Paul carried out an investigation to find out which colour of petals bees prefer. He put four pots of dahlia flowers in the same place in the garden. Each pot contained flowers of the same colour. For 30 minutes he recorded the number of times bees visited each pot.

His results are shown opposite.

Colour	Number of visits
white	10
red	19
yellow	25
pink	15

(a) Why did Paul use the same type of flower in each pot?

____ 1 mark

(b) According to Paul's results, which colour do bees prefer?

____ 1 mark

(c) Paul thinks he should repeat his investigation a second time, using the same flowers to check his results. Which other factor should Paul keep the same?

____

____ 1 mark

(d) Do you think Paul will get exactly the same results when he repeats his investigation? Explain your answer.

____

__________________________ 1 mark

TOTAL

How did you score?

4 or less – try again!
5 or 6 – nearly there!
7 or 8 – well done!

PLANT GROWTH

What you need to know

1 Know that a plant needs certain conditions for it to grow healthily.

2 Know that a plant will die if these conditions are not met.

3 Know that plants make their own food.

GROWING CONDITIONS

- A plant needs air, light, heat, **nutrients** and water to grow well.
- A plant is able to take **carbon dioxide** from the air, and with water and light, create sugar for food and **oxygen**.
- If plants are not kept in good conditions they will not grow well and will eventually die.

Jack took four pots, filled them with soil and planted one seed in each. He put each pot into a different place and looked after it in a different way to see how well each one grew.

This is a healthy plant. It has green leaves and upright stems. It was kept in a warm, bright place and watered regularly.

This plant has dried-up leaves and a weak stem. It was kept in a warm, bright place but was not watered at all.

This plant has a thin, spindly stem and yellow leaves. It was watered regularly but kept in a dark place. Its leaves are yellow because the plant could not produce its food.

This seed did not produce a plant. It was kept in the fridge. The temperature was too cold for the seed to germinate and start to grow.

MAKING FOOD

- The roots of a **plant** take up water and nutrients from the soil and also **anchor** the plant.
- The **stem** carries water and nutrients.
- The **leaves** create the plant's food and get rid of carbon dioxide.

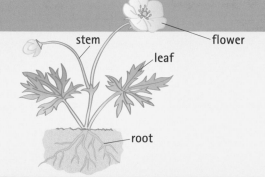

stem

flower

leaf

root

PLANT GROWTH

1 Ashley is growing two trays of cress. She leaves one tray on the windowsill in the kitchen and she puts the other tray into a dark cupboard. Over the next three weeks she regularly waters both trays.

(a) Through which part of the plant does the cress take in water?

1 mark

(b) What do you think the cress plants that were kept in the cupboard would look like after three weeks?

_____

_____

1 mark

(c) What was the purpose of Ashley's experiment?

_____

1 mark

(d) Ashley notices that the grass in her garden does not grow in the winter? Give **TWO** factors which could affect how the grass grows.

(i) _____

(ii) _____

2 marks

(e) Ashley has also been growing a sunflower in her garden. Which piece of equipment is she using to measure the height of the sunflower?

_____

1 mark

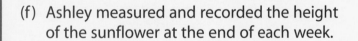

(f) Ashley measured and recorded the height of the sunflower at the end of each week.

She has put her results into a table but she has made a mistake.
What is the mistake in Ashley's results?

_____

1 mark

End of week	Height (cm)
1	90
2	120
3	138
4	136
5	170
6	183

(g) Suggest what this value could have been.

_____

1 mark

TOTAL

PLANT GROWTH INVESTIGATION

Investigate some of the factors which affect plant growth.

You will need
three small green plants, for example, pansies
a pencil

If the plants are not in individual pots, then ask an adult to help you to put them each into their own pot with some soil or compost.

What to do

1 Label the pots A, B and C.

2 Put Plant A on a bright windowsill, but not in direct sunlight. Water this plant every two days making sure that the soil is moist but not soggy. There should be no water lying on the top of the soil.

3 Put Plant B on the same windowsill. Do not water this plant at all.

4 Put Plant C into a dark cupboard. Water this plant every two days making sure that the soil is moist but not soggy.

5 Predict what you think will have happened to each plant after one and two weeks. Write your predictions in the table below.

	After 1 week		After 2 weeks	
	Prediction	Actual	Prediction	Actual
Plant A				
Plant B				
Plant C				

Now answer the questions on page 44.

1 After one week write down what you actually see. Do the same again after two weeks.

How do your predictions compare with the actual results?

_____

_____

_____

_____

_____

2 What did you do to ensure you made this a fair test? Write **THREE** things.

(i) _____

_____

(ii) _____

_____

(iii) _____

_____

3 What can you say about the factors needed for good plant growth?

_____

_____

HABITATS AND ADAPTATION

What you need to know

1 Know that different plants and animals are found in different environments (habitats).

2 Understand how animals and plants are adapted to their habitats by their different features.

HABITATS

- A **habitat** is a place where a plant or animal lives. Habitats may be large or small, for example a desert or a garden pond.
- Animals and plants are suited to live in their habitats, and would not be suited to live in all environments.
- Humans have to **adapt** to whatever climate or **environment** they find themselves in, otherwise they would become too hot or too cold and would not be able to function properly.

ADAPTING TO HABITATS

- Some animals are specially adapted to their habitats:

a heron has a sharp beak to catch fish, a kestrel has talons to grip branches and catch prey, a polar bear has thick fur to keep it warm and a fish has gills so that it can breathe underwater.

This garden shows the habitats of some animals and plants and how they adapt to them.

thrush
It lives in bushes and trees where it is well-camouflaged and lives on insects, snails, worms and berries which are all available in the garden.

garden spider
It lives on the hedge as there are lots of places to attach its web and lots of insects around to trap in it.

fern
It doesn't need much light so it lives in a shady part of garden.

earthworm
It lives on and in the soil and has bristles to help it move through the soil. It eats the soil as it burrows.

frog
It spends time in the pond when laying eggs so has webbed feet to help it swim. It also lives around the pond where it catches insects with its tongue.

marsh marigold
Its roots like to be in wet soil so it lives next to the pond.

woodlouse
It has a flat shell and feeds on decaying leaves so it lives under stones and rotting wood.

HABITATS AND ADAPTATION

1 A group of children are studying the plants and animals in the school wildlife garden.

Put a tick next to the living things which the children are most likely to find in the wildlife garden.

woodlouse ☐	jellyfish ☐	red admiral butterfly ☐
daisy ☐	cactus ☐	parrot ☐
slug ☐	starfish ☐	

2 marks

2 A frog is an animal which lives in and around the pond in the garden.

Describe **TWO** ways in which a frog is adapted to its habitat.

(i) _____

(ii) _____

2 marks

3 One of the children has noticed that there are lots of dandelions growing in the grassy part of the garden.

Describe **TWO** features of the dandelion which help it to survive in the garden.

(i) _____

(ii) _____

2 marks

4 The children collect 10 woodlice from under a damp stone in the corner of the garden. Then the children are given the items shown opposite.

cardboard tray

clear plastic tray

cling film

black card

water spray

sand

soil

Describe how the children could use some of these items to build a suitable habitat in the classroom in which to keep the woodlice.

_____

_____

_____

2 marks

TOTAL ☐

How did you score?

4 or less – try again!
5 or 6 – nearly there!
7 or 8 – well done!

FOOD CHAINS

What you need to know

1 Understand that most food chains start with a green plant.

2 Know the terms producer, consumer, prey and predator.

3 Understand that if one part of a food chain alters, this affects the whole chain.

WHO EATS WHAT?

- Everything we eat and everything that other living things eat is linked.
- Every living thing relies on a group of plants or animals for its food.
- These links between plants and animals are called **food chains**. Most food chains start with a green plant:

> marigold → snail → thrush → cat

WHO'S WHO?

- All plants are **producers** because they make their own food.
- All animals are **consumers** because they eat other plants and animals.

> a weasel eats only other animals, e.g. mice and birds
> a rabbit eats mainly grass and the roots of some plants and trees
> a thrush eats snails, worms and insects as well as berries and fruits

- A **predator** is an animal which gets its food by eating other animals. The animals that predators eat are called **prey**.

> a kestrel will kill and eat a fieldmouse
> a fox will kill and eat a rabbit
> a blackbird will kill and eat an earthworm

CHANGING CHAINS

- An animal or plant can be part of more than one food chain.

> rose → **greenfly** → ladybird
> lupin → **greenfly** → frog → heron

What would happen if one part of the food chain was changed? Gardeners treat snails as a pest because they eat the leaves of many plants. There are not enough thrushes to kill the snails so gardeners have to use other, less environmentally-friendly, ways to get rid of them. Nature experts think that one of the reasons that there aren't enough thrushes is the growing number of cats which are killing them. If the cat was removed from the food chain there would be more thrushes to control the number of snails.

FOOD CHAINS

1 Some of these plants and animals are predators, some are prey and the rest are producers.

grass	spider	fly	fox	rabbit
blackbird	lettuce	algae	tadpole	

(a) Complete the table by putting each plant or animal into the correct column.

producer	prey	predator

2 marks

(b) From the table of plants and animals above, complete two different food chains.

______ → ______ ______

1 mark

______ → ______ ______

1 mark

2 Here are three food chains linked together. This is called a food web.

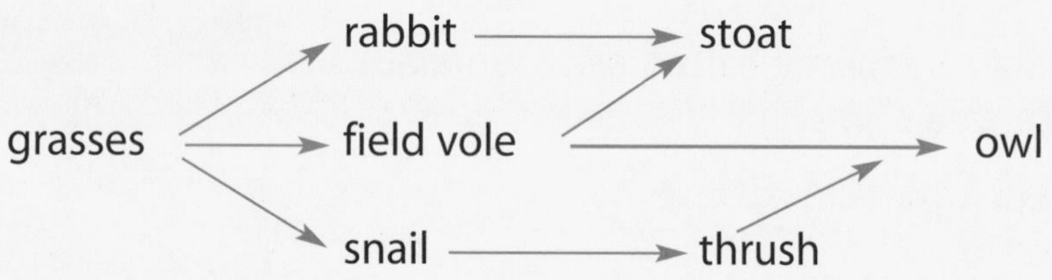

rabbit
stoat
grasses
field vole
owl
snail
thrush

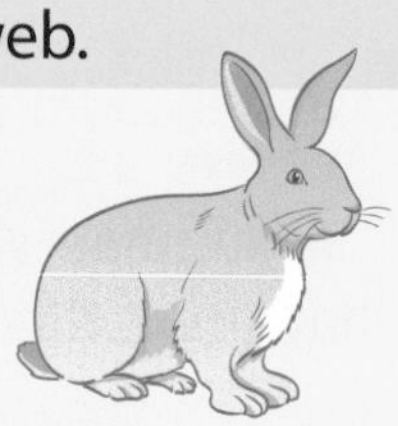

(a) What would be the effect on the food web if there were less grasses than usual one year?

____

____

2 marks

(b) What would be the effect on the food web if there were more owls born than usual one year?

____

____

2 marks

TOTAL

How did you score?

4 or less – try again!
5 or 6 – nearly there!
7 or 8 – well done!

HEALTH

What you need to know

1 Know that different foods do different jobs in the human body.

2 Understand the importance of a balanced and varied diet to a healthy lifestyle.

3 Know that smoking, alcohol and some drugs can be damaging.

FOOD JOBS

- The four main food groups are:

carbohydrates   proteins   fats   vitamins and minerals

Food group	How the body uses them	Found in
carbohydrates	give the body energy	cereals, potatoes, bread, pasta, sugar
proteins	build up the body and help to repair cells	fish, meat, eggs, dairy produce, lentils, nuts
fats	give the body energy which it then stores	butter, cheese, sausages, bacon
vitamins and minerals	help the body to grow and stay healthy, build bones and teeth and help muscles work	fruit, vegetables, fish, meat, cheese, milk

- A healthy **balanced diet** contains foods from all four groups in the right amounts. A balanced meal could include a piece of chicken, boiled potatoes, peas and carrots followed by a banana and custard.
- Some foods also contain **fibre**. It is needed to help digest food and move it through the digestive system. Fibre is found in bread, cereals, fruit and vegetables.
- Many foods and all drinks contain **water** which is also very important.

HARMFUL DRUGS

- **Smoking** is bad for your health because the **tar** in cigarettes damages the lungs. **Nicotine** is the drug found in cigarettes that makes them addictive. Smoking near other people can cause them harm.
- Too much **alcohol** damages the liver and brain and slows the reactions.
- Some other **drugs** can be harmful.

1 Beth and Jane are eating lunch in the dining hall. The pictures show what each has for their lunch.

Beth   **Jane**

(a) Describe **ONE** way in which Beth's lunch is not healthy.

_____   1 mark

(b) Describe **ONE** way in which Jane's lunch is healthy.

_____   1 mark

(c) At break time Jane drinks a small carton of milk.
Tick **ONE** box which explains why milk is an important food.

It contains fibre to help digest food. ☐   It increases your heart rate. ☐

It contains calcium for strong bones ☐   It tastes sweet. ☐   1 mark
and teeth.

(d) Jane is making a poster about having a healthy lifestyle.

Write **THREE** more ideas which Jane could include on her poster.

> **Ways for a healthly lifestyle**
>
> • Don't drink too much alcohol.
>
> (i) _____
>
> (ii) _____
>
> (iii) _____

3 marks

(e) Jane has included the statement 'Don't drink too much alcohol' on her poster. Alcohol slows down the time it takes to react. Why do you think it is important not to drink alcohol before driving a car?

_____   1 mark

(f) Beth says, 'All drugs are bad for you'.
Do you agree with Beth?   Circle   **Yes**   or   **No**
Explain your answer giving a reason.

_____

_____   1 mark

TOTAL ☐

How did you score?

4 or less – try again!
5 or 6 – nearly there!
7 or 8 – well done!

50

HEART AND EXERCISE

What you need to know

1 Know that the heart is a muscle.

2 Understand the function of the heart.

3 Know that oxygen is carried in the blood.

4 Understand the effects of exercise and rest on pulse rate.

5 Know how to keep a heart healthy.

THE HEART

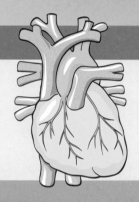

- The **heart** is a powerful muscle which pumps blood around the body.
- Regular exercise and healthy eating help to keep the heart and blood vessels healthy.
- Smoking, lack of exercise and fatty foods can lead to an unhealthy heart and blood vessels.

BLOOD

- Blood **circulates** around the body through **blood vessels**.
- The different types of blood vessels are: **arteries**, **veins** and **capillaries**.
- Through the process of **breathing** (**respiration**), **oxygen** is taken into the blood and **carbon dioxide** is removed from it.

PULSE AND EXERCISE

- Your **pulse** is a measurement of your heart rate.
- Your pulse is measured as the number of beats your heart makes in one minute.
- When you exercise, your muscles need more oxygen very quickly so you breathe faster to take in more oxygen. Your heart then works harder to get the oxygen to the muscles which are doing the exercise. This is why your pulse rate increases. As soon as you stop and rest, your pulse starts to decrease.

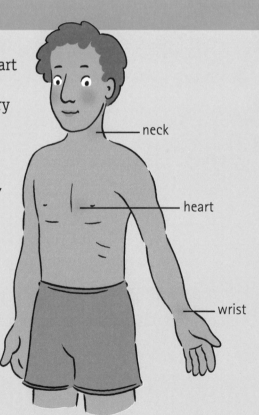

neck

heart

wrist

These are the different points on the body where you can feel your pulse more strongly.

HEART AND EXERCISE

1 Helen wanted to know how her pulse rate changed after doing different activities. After each activity she rested and measured her pulse rate at three different times.

(a What does pulse rate measure? _____ 1 mark

Her results are shown below.

Activity	Pulse rate (beats per minute)		
	Just after activity	2 minutes after activity	15 minutes after activity
Resting	70	70	70
Working at desk	72	72	71
Slow jogging	125	100	72
Running	171	115	71

(b) Tick **ONE** box to show how Helen's results are presented.

bar chart ☐   pictogram ☐   graph ☐   table ☐   1 mark

(c) What was Helen's pulse rate 2 minutes after she stopped running?   [beats per minute]   1 mark

(d) Explain why Helen's pulse rate stayed the same when she had only been resting.

_____   1 mark

(e) Explain why Helen's pulse rate was higher when she was jogging and running.

_____   1 mark

(f) What do you notice about Helen's pulse rate 15 minutes after each activity?

_____   1 mark

(g) What do you think her pulse rate would be 20 minutes after jogging?   [   ]   1 mark

(h) Helen noticed that when her doctor measured her pulse rate he only counted the number of beats for 10 seconds. How could the doctor use this to work out the number of beats per minute?

_____   1 mark

TOTAL [   ]

PULSE RATE INVESTIGATION

Investigate the effect of exercise on pulse rate.

You will need
a stopwatch
or a watch with a second hand

What to do

1 You are going to do four different activities each for exactly five minutes and then measure your pulse rate immediately after each one.

The four activities are:
sit still   walk slowly   walk briskly   jog

2 As soon as you have timed yourself doing each activity for 5 minutes, start to measure your pulse rate. Count the number of beats for 10 seconds only.

3 Record your results in the table below in the 1st attempt columns.

4 Then multiply this number by 6 to get the number of beats per minute which is your pulse rate.

Pulse points

Look back at page 51 to find the best places on your body for measuring the pulse rate.

Activity	1st attempt		2nd attempt	
	number of beats in 10 seconds	number of beats in 1 minute	number of beats in 10 seconds	number of beats in 1 minute
Sitting				
Walking slowly				
Walking briskly				
Jogging				

5 Repeat the whole investigation again and this time record your observations in the 2nd attempt columns.

Now answer the questions on page 54.

1 Why is it important to repeat the experiment?

_____

_____

2 Which factor has been kept constant in each activity?

_____

3 Why is it important to measure your pulse immediately after the activity rather than some time later?

_____

4 What do your observations tell you about pulse rate and exercise?

_____

_____

_____

_____

5 Regular exercise helps to keep the heart healthy, however, exercise also has other benefits. Find out about and write down four other things which exercise is good for.

(i) _____

(ii) _____

(iii) _____

(iv) _____

TEETH

What you need to know

1 Know how teeth develop as we grow older.

2 Name and recognize the three types of teeth and what they do.

3 Know what causes tooth decay and how to prevent it.

GROWING TEETH

- **Babies** do not need teeth as they only drink milk and eat soft foods.

- **Children** grow a set of 20 milk teeth.

- **Adults** develop a set of 32 permanent teeth.

TYPES OF TEETH

- The three types of teeth are:

   incisor for snipping and cutting

   canine for tearing and ripping

  molar for chewing and grinding.

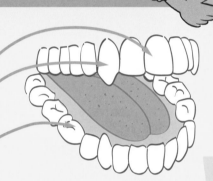

TOOTH DECAY

- Sugar in food attracts bacteria in the mouth and produces plaque on the teeth.
- Plaque produces an acid which attacks tooth enamel, causing decay.

Big and Sharp

Carnivores need strong, sharp canines to kill and tear the meat off their prey. **Herbivores** need sharp incisors to bite fruit and leaves as well as large molars to grind their food.

Mr I Pullem (FRCDS)
DENTAL SURGEON

To prevent tooth decay: brush your teeth twice a day. Visit your dentist regularly.

★★★★★★★★★★★★★★
Remember
Calcium is needed for strong teeth. Keep drinking milk!
★★★★★★★★★★★★★★

TEETH

1 Rebecca has been for a check-up at her dentist's surgery. Her dentist is concerned that she needs a filling and is not brushing her teeth properly. The dentist shows Rebecca a model of a set of teeth to point out the tooth which he needs to fill.

(a) Name the type of tooth shown by the arrow.

_____ 1 mark

(b) What is the function of this type of tooth?

_____ 1 mark

2 The dentist has given Rebecca seven special tablets to chew each night after she has brushed her teeth. The tablets will stain any plaque left on her teeth purple.

(a) Tick **ONE** box to show which word best describes what Rebecca is doing?

an observation ☐   an effect ☐   a measurement ☐   a question ☐   1 mark

(b) Why do you think the dentist has asked her to do this seven times?

_____ 1 mark

3 Study this graph showing the level of plaque on Rebecca's teeth at different times of the day.

(a) Why do you think the plaque level has fallen at points A and B?

_____ 2 marks

(b) Give **TWO** ways in which Rebecca could take better care of her teeth.

(i) _____

(ii) _____ 2 marks

TOTAL ☐

SKELETON AND MUSCLES

What you need to know

1 Understand the main functions of the skeleton.

2 Know how bones are joined.

3 Start to understand how some muscles work.

THE SKELETON

- The **skeleton** has three main functions: **protection**, **support** and **movement**.

  The skeleton protects vital organs:
  the **skull** protects the brain
  the **rib** cage protects the heart and lungs
  the **spine** protects the spinal cord.

  The skeleton supports the soft
  parts of the body; without it
  the body would collapse.

  The skeleton allows movement such
  as walking, running and throwing.

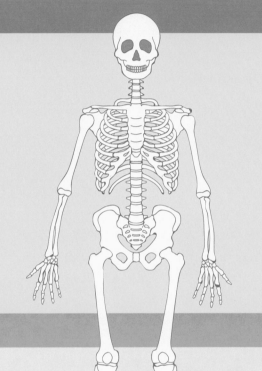

BONES

- Bones are joined by joints.

  Two types of **joints** are hinge joints,
  (for example the elbow and knee) and
  ball and socket joints, (for example
  the hip and shoulder).

- **Cartilage** protects the ends of the
  bones and allows them to move easily.

MUSCLES

- **Muscles** are attached to the bones of the
  skeleton and the muscles move the bones
  by **contracting** and **expanding**.
- Muscles can only pull, they cannot push.
- Muscles usually work in pairs, for example
  the triceps and biceps in the arms.

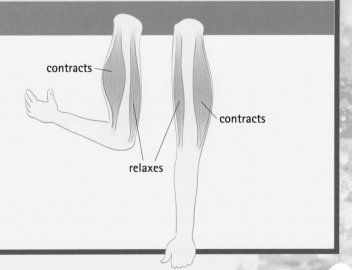

contracts

contracts

relaxes

SKELETON AND MUSCLES

1 (a) Mark has broken a bone in his arm.
What is the medical word used for a broken bone?

_____ 1 mark

(b) The doctor puts a plaster cast on Mark's arm.
Tick **TWO** reasons for doing this.

It keeps the bone in place. ☐

It prevents infection. ☐

It keeps the bone clean. ☐

It protects the bone from knocks. ☐   2 marks

(c) After a few weeks Mark has his cast removed.
He notices that his arm feels weaker.
Why does his arm feel weaker?

_____

_____ 1 mark

2 Some of the bones in the human skeleton are designed to protect important organs.
Draw lines to match the bones in the skeleton to the labels showing the organs they protect.

brain

heart and lungs

spinal cord

3 marks

3 The shoulder is an example of a ball and socket joint.

Name another joint which works in the same way as the shoulder.

_____ 1 mark

TOTAL ☐

HUMAN LIFE CYCLE

What you need to know

1 Understand the human life cycle and the changes that occur.

2 Know that reproduction is an essential part of this cycle.

LIFE CYCLE CHANGES

The human life cycle

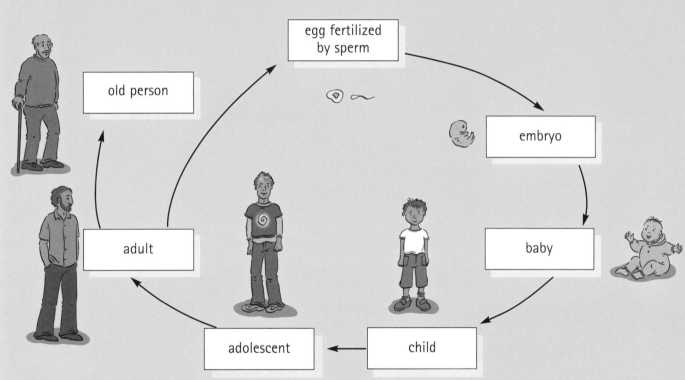

REPRODUCTION

- An **egg** from the mother is **fertilized** by a **sperm** from the father and grows into an embryo.
- The **embryo** develops into a **baby** inside the mother. After about nine months the baby is born.
- The baby develops and grows into a **child**.
- **Puberty** happens when the child grows into an **adolescent**. This is when the body develops into an **adult** body.
- Adults are able to reproduce and continue the life cycle.

HUMAN LIFE CYCLE

1 (a) Complete the missing stages of the human life cycle.

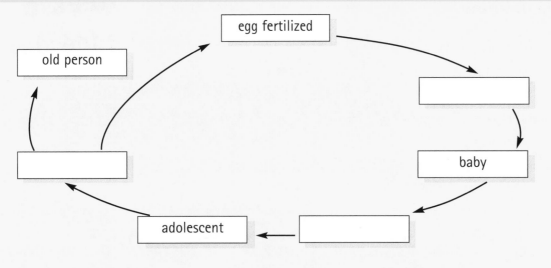

3 marks

(b) At which stage does puberty occur? _____ 1 mark

(c) About how long does it take for a baby to fully grow inside its mother?

3 months ☐   9 months ☐   1 year ☐   2 years ☐   1 mark

(d) Why don't very young babies need teeth?

_____ 1 mark

(e) Babies start to learn about different sounds, colours and textures from an early age.

Here is a toy designed for a baby.

Describe **TWO** ways in which the toy would help a baby to learn new skills.

(i) _____

_____

(ii) _____

_____ 2 marks

TOTAL ☐

MICRO-ORGANISMS

What you need to know

1 Know that micro-organisms are very small living things.

2 Know that micro-organisms can be helpful or harmful.

3 Know how to reduce the spread of harmful micro-organisms.

MICRO-SIZED LIVING THINGS

- **Micro-organisms** are very small living things; they are so small that they can only be seen through a powerful microscope.
- Micro-organisms are found in food, water and air, as well as on and inside the bodies of humans and animals.

HELPFUL OR HARMFUL?

- Some micro-organisms are harmful.
- Many of the illnesses and infections that humans suffer from are caused by micro-organisms.

The common cold is caused by a type of micro-organism called a **virus**. Plaque contains **bacteria**, another type of micro-organism, which causes tooth decay. **Mould** is a type of micro-organism found on decaying food which can cause illness if eaten.

- Some micro-organisms are helpful.

Yeast is a micro-organism which is used to make bread. Yoghurt also contains a helpful bacteria.

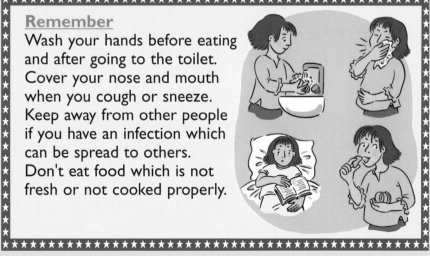

- Some micro-organisms cause dead plants and animals to decay. This might not sound too good but it is a very important job.

REDUCE THE SPREAD OF HARMFUL MICRO-ORGANISMS

- It is very important that we take steps to avoid spreading harmful micro-organisms.

<u>Remember</u>
Wash your hands before eating and after going to the toilet. Cover your nose and mouth when you cough or sneeze. Keep away from other people if you have an infection which can be spread to others. Don't eat food which is not fresh or not cooked properly.

MICRO-ORGANISMS

1 Louis Pasteur was a chemist who was born in 1822. He helped to find the link between germs and disease. A germe is an example of:

a material ☐   a micro-organism ☐   a food ☐   an acid ☐   1 mark

2 Pasteur was asked to investigate why some barrels of beer had gone sour. He took a sample from several barrels. Then he studied the samples in his laboratory.

(a) What is meant by a sample?

_____   1 mark

(b) Why did Pasteur take a sample of beer from several barrels and not just one?

_____   1 mark

(c) Which piece of equipment do you think Pasteur used to study the samples?

magnifying glass ☐   microscope ☐   scales ☐   computer ☐   1 mark

3 Pasteur also found a cure for a disease in chickens. He tested the cure on one group of chickens and recorded his results. He then repeated his test on another group of chickens.

Why do you think Pasteur repeated his test?

_____   1 mark

4 Scientists who work with germs and diseases wear masks and gloves.

Why do you think this is sensible?

_____   1 mark

5 Barry buys a loaf of bread. He leaves it in a warm cupboard for two weeks.

(a) What will have happened to the bread after two weeks?

_____   1 mark

(b) How could Barry have kept the bread fresh?

_____   1 mark

TOTAL ☐

How did you score?

4 or less – try again!
5 or 6 – nearly there!
7 or 8 – well done!

HEALTHY EATING INVESTIGATION

Healthy eating experts recommend that everyone should eat at least five portions of fruit and vegetables a day.

Investigate whether you and your friends or family are eating enough fruit and vegetables.

First of all you need to know what is meant by a 'portion' of fruit or vegetables.
Here are some examples of one portion:
- a glass of orange juice
- an apple or banana
- two rings of tinned pineappple
- three large spoonfuls of peas, sweetcorn or baked beans
- a small bowl of salad

What to do

1 Use the tally chart below to record the number of portions each person eats on the same day (add more rows if you need to).

Name	Number of servings of fruit and vegetables	
	Tally	Total

2 Display your results by completing the bar chart below.

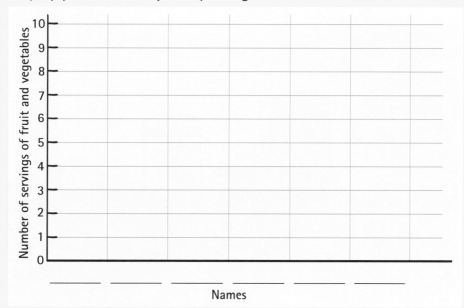

Now answer the questions on page 64.

1 What is your conclusion?

_____

_____

_____

_____

2 Do you think you have collected enough data?
Give a reason for your answer.

_____

_____

_____

_____

3 How could you improve your results?

_____

_____

_____

_____

PROPERTIES OF MATERIALS

What you need to know

1 Know that some materials occur naturally and some are manufactured.

2 Understand that materials have particular properties that make them special and useful for different jobs.

NATURAL OR MANUFACTURED?

- Some materials are **natural**, such as oil, granite, sandstone, diamond, slate, clay, iron, silver, wood, leather, wool, silk and cotton.
- Other materials are **manufactured**, such as nylon, Lycra, fibre glass, polythene, PVC and Perspex.

PROPERTIES

- Materials have **properties**, or special features, which make them useful for different jobs.

Property	Materials	Used for	Opposite
Transparent (can see through it)	glass, Perspex	windows, lights, greenhouses, bottles	Materials which cannot be seen through are **opaque**.
Waterproof (does not soak up water)	plastics, metals, nylon	cars, garden furniture, umbrellas	Materials which do soak up water are **absorbent**.
Strong (difficult to break)	steel, concrete, wood	buildings, bridges, furniture	Materials which are easy to break are **brittle**.
Flexible (easy to bend)	plastic, rubber, leather	hosepipes, shoes, tyres	Materials which are not easy to bend are **rigid**.
Hard (difficult to scratch)	granite, diamond, some metals	floors, cutting tools, machine tools	Materials which are easy to scratch are **soft**.

Parts of this car are made from different materials depending on the job they are designed to do.

fabric covered foam chairs: soft and comfortable

toughened glass windscreen: can be seen through and will not shatter in an accident

steel body: strong and easy to mould into shape

plastic bumper: quite soft to reduce damage in an accident

rubber tyres: soft and flexible to grip the road and make driving more comfortable

PROPERTIES OF MATERIALS

1 Look at this chart. Ameena has been testing the properties of materials to see which materials would be good for making an umbrella.

Her results are shown opposite.

Material	Transparent	Strong	Waterproof	Light
Cotton	✗	✔	✗	✔
Clear polythene	✔	✔	✔	✔
Tissue paper	✗	✗	✗	✔
Kitchen foil	✗	✔	✔	✔
Perspex	✔	✔	✔	✔

(a) Which materials were both transparent and waterproof?

2 marks

(b) Why would cotton not be a good material to use for an umbrella?

_____

1 mark

(c) Which material might Ameena have thought was best for an umbrella, and why?

_____

2 marks

2 Laura has just bought a new pair of trainers for running.

Zoom3
is the latest in running footwear. It is guaranteed to improve your speed when running on any surface. *Zoom3* features a reflective patch on the heel and toe cap, a thick rubber sole and waterproof fabric upper.

reflective heel patch

waterproof fabric upper

reflective toe patch

rubber sole

zoom 3

Why do you think that each of these features has been included in the design of the shoe?

reflective patches _____ *1 mark*

rubber sole _____ *1 mark*

waterproof fabric _____ *1 mark*

TOTAL [ ]

SOLIDS, LIQUIDS, GASES

What you need to know

1 Know that materials can exist in three different forms: solid, liquid and gas.

2 Know the characteristics of each state of matter.

3 Be able to identify and categorize a substance as being solid, liquid or gas.

4 Understand that heating and cooling may change substances from one state of matter to another.

THREE FORMS OF MATERIALS

- All materials can be classified as being a **solid**, a **liquid** or a **gas**.

Solid	Liquid	Gas
chocolate	washing-up liquid	helium
nail	water	steam
CD	syrup	natural gas
sock	milk	carbon dioxide

IDENTIFYING CHARACTERISTICS

- **Solids** can be held. They have a definite shape and they can keep this shape. They keep the same volume. Solids can be cut or shaped.

- **Liquids** flow downward. They take up the shape of the container they are in and find their own level. Liquids may be poured. They are not easy to hold.

- **Gases** are often invisible. They do not flow. They fill up empty spaces or the container they are in. They have no definite volume. A mixture of gases, in the form of air, is all around us.

helium-filled balloon

steam

> **Tricky solids!**
> Sand, flour and other powders are solids. Each particle stays the same shape and volume.

HEATING AND COOLING

- If we **heat** a solid, we may be able to change it into a liquid or a gas.
- If we **cool** a gas, we may be able to change it into a liquid or a solid.

At room temperature water is a liquid. If it is heated it changes into a gas (**water vapour**); if cooled it changes into a solid (**ice**).

SOLIDS, LIQUIDS, GASES

1 Ellie has a bottle of cola.

(a) Complete the labels using the words:
solid, liquid, gas.

(b) Ellie leaves the top off the bottle for several
hours. She pours some of the cola into a glass.
The cola is no longer fizzy.

What happened to make the cola no longer fizzy?

3 marks

_____

_____ 1 mark

2 Asim is testing different liquids.
He has four cylinders, each containing
a different liquid. He drops a marble
into each cylinder and times how
long it takes the marble to fall to
the bottom.

water	washing-up liquid	syrup	wallpaper paste
time taken 2 seconds	time taken 7 seconds	time taken 20 seconds	time taken 30 seconds

(a) Which liquid property is Asim testing?

colour ☐   thickness ☐   smell ☐   stickiness ☐   1 mark

(b) What conclusion can you draw using the results of Asim's test?

_____ 1 mark

3 Kylie has two balloons. One is filled with air and the other is filled with a
gas called helium. She notices that the balloon filled with helium floats up
to the ceiling and the balloon filled with air lies on the floor.

(a) What do her observations tell you about the gas helium?

1 mark

_____

(b) She bursts the balloon filled with helium with a pin.
Where does the helium go?

_____ 1 mark

TOTAL ☐

How did
you score?

4 or less – try again!
5 or 6 – nearly there!
7 or 8 – well done!

REVERSIBLE CHANGES

What you need to know

1 Know that heating, cooling and mixing can cause physical changes.

2 Know that some physical changes to materials can be reversed.

3 Know that the water cycle is an example of a reversible change.

4 Know that evaporation and condensation are changes in the water cycle.

CHANGING MATERIALS

- Some materials can be changed by heating and cooling.
- Some changes can be **reversed** and are called **reversible changes**.

melting a **solid** turns it into a **liquid**

evaporating a liquid turns it into a **gas**

condensing a gas turns it into a liquid

freezing a liquid turns it into a solid

- Some solids can be mixed with liquids.
  In some cases these changes can be reversed (*see Week 8 Monday*).

WATER CYCLE

- The **water cycle** is an example of a reversible change.

Water vapour evaporates from the sea, rivers and lakes as the sun heats it.

As the water vapour rises, it cools and condenses to form clouds.

The clouds cool and water droplets are formed.

The water droplets fall back into the sea, rivers or lakes as rain.

REVERSIBLE CHANGES

1 Here are the four stages of the water cycle.
They are not in the correct order.

    A   clouds cool to form water droplets
    B   clouds are formed by water vapour condensing
    C   water droplets fall as rain into seas and rivers
    D   water evaporates from seas and rivers

(a) Write a letter in each box in the diagram opposite to show the correct order of the stages in the water cycle.

2 marks

(b) Tick **ONE** box to show what change happens during condensation.

solid changes to liquid ☐   solid changes to gas ☐

gas changes to liquid ☐   liquid changes to gas ☐

1 mark

(c) The types of changes which occur in the water cycle are reversible.
What is meant by reversible?

_____ 1 mark

(d) Give a different example of a reversible change.

_____ 1 mark

2 (a) Scott takes a container out of the freezer. It contains frozen soup. He takes the frozen block of soup out of the container and puts it into a pan. Scott then puts the pan on a low heat on the cooker.

What starts to happen to the block of soup?

_____ 1 mark

(b) After heating it gently for a few minutes he notices that steam starts to rise from the pan. What does this suggest is happening to the soup?

_____ 1 mark

(c) Scott heats the soup in the pan for 10 minutes. The soup is now ready to eat. What would happen if he kept heating the soup for an hour?

_____ 1 mark

TOTAL ☐

How did you score?

4 or less – try again!
5 or 6 – nearly there!
7 or 8 – well done!

NON-REVERSIBLE CHANGES

What you need to know

1 Know that heating, cooling and mixing some materials can cause physical changes.

2 Know that some physical changes to materials cannot be reversed. These are called non-reversible changes.

3 Recognize some everyday non-reversible changes.

MAKING CHANGES

- Some materials can be changed by heating, cooling and mixing.
- Some of these changes can be reversed.

If a bar of chocolate is warmed, it melts but it can be made **solid** again by cooling it.

PERMANENT CHANGES

- Heating other materials changes them permanently. It is impossible to get back the materials used in their original form. These are **non-reversible** changes and cannot be reversed.

If an egg is warmed it starts to change; the clear part of the egg starts to turn white as it begins to cook.

- If some materials are heated for longer, or at higher temperatures, they burn. The changes that occur cannot be reversed.

If the bar of chocolate is heated in a pan at a high temperature, it will first melt but then start to burn. Once it has started to burn, the chocolate cannot return to its original form.

- Other non-reversible changes can happen when some solids are mixed with some **liquids**.

If plaster of Paris is mixed with water, it forms a thick liquid which then sets into a solid. This change is non-reversible.

When vinegar and bicarbonate of soda are mixed together changes occur which cannot be reversed.

However, there are some mixtures which can be reversed: (*see Week 8 Monday*).

Good Luck! ♡
x x x

NON-REVERSIBLE CHANGES

1 Ian is making a birthday cake. He makes the cake mixture by mixing together butter, flour, sugar and eggs in a bowl using an electric mixer.

(a) Which of the ingredients can he get back out of the mixture?

all of them ☐   only butter ☐

none of them ☐   butter and eggs ☐

1 mark

(b) Which word best describes the type of change that has taken place?

☐

1 mark

(c) Ian puts the cake mixture into a baking tin and bakes it in the oven for 30 minutes. What would happen to the cake if he baked it for 3 hours?

1 mark

(d) Ian wants to coat the top of the cake with chocolate.
He gently warms some pieces of chocolate in a bowl.
What change happens to the chocolate?

1 mark

(e) How will this change help Ian to put the chocolate on the top of the cake?

1 mark

(f) When the cake is finished Ian puts some candles on it. He lights the candles with a match and notices that as the candles burn they all get shorter. Which word in the last sentence suggests that this change is permanent?

☐

1 mark

(g) Which word describes what Ian is doing?

observation ☐   experiment ☐   survey ☐   plan ☐

1 mark

(h) What will have happened to the match after Ian used it to light the candles?

1 mark

TOTAL ☐

EVAPORATION INVESTIGATION

Water evaporates (turns into a gas) when it is warmed.

Investigate how long it takes water to evaporate at different temperatures.

You will need to put some water in containers and then put each one in a different place around your home (inside and outside if possible) making sure you choose a cold place, a cool place and a warm place. For example, the airing cupboard will be warmer than inside the garage.

Here is some equipment which you could use for this investigation:

1 Tick the items you think you will need.

2 Now find these items in your home.

3 Choose three places in your home which have different temperatures.

4 Write them here.

1	2

3

You now need to set up your equipment.

5 Put a container of water in each place and check it at regular intervals for the next seven days.

Now answer the questions on page 74.

1 Explain how you will ensure you are carrying out the test fairly.

_____

_____

_____

2 Record your observations using the table below.

For each container, on each day put a tick in the box if there is still some water left and put a cross if there is no water left.

Place	Day 1	Day 2	Day 3	Day 4	Day 5	Day 6	Day 7
1							
2							
3							

Write a conclusion about your observations.

_____

_____

_____

_____

METHODS OF SEPARATION

What you need to know

1 Know that some solids and liquids can be mixed together and then be separated.

2 Know that those mixtures which can be separated are examples of reversible changes.

3 Know the main methods of separation and which method applies to which type of mixture.

SEPARATION FACTS

- A **mixture** made up of solid **particles**, for example, sand and pebbles, may be **separated** by **sieving**.
- Solid particles mixed with a liquid, for example, sand in water, can be separated by **filtering**.
- Some solids can **dissolve** in water (or other liquids) to make a **solution**, for example, salt or sugar in water. The solid can be separated from the liquid by **evaporation**. Solids which dissolve in liquids are called **soluble**.
- There is a limit to the amount of solid which can dissolve into a given amount of liquid.
- Iron and steel materials are **magnetic** and may be separated from a mixture of solid materials using a magnet.

SEPARATION METHODS

- These mixtures can be separated in different ways. They are examples of reversible changes.

A mixture of rice grains and flour can be separated using a sieve.

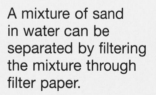

A mixture of sand in water can be separated by filtering the mixture through filter paper.

A solution of salt in water can be separated by boiling the solution until all the water has evaporated. The salt will be left as a solid in the dish. (The water could be collected by letting the water vapour condense into water droplets on a cold surface.)

A mixture of plastic and steel paperclips can be separated by using a magnet to attract the steel paperclips, leaving the plastic ones behind.

METHODS OF SEPARATION

1 Amy has been told that salt will dissolve in water to form a solution.
She puts 200 cm³ of water into a beaker.
Amy then adds one teaspoon of salt and it dissolves.

(a) What could she do to the water to make the salt dissolves more quickly?

_____   1 mark

(b) What will eventually happen if she keeps adding more teaspoonfuls of salt to the solution?

_____   1 mark

(c) Amy now pours the mixture through a filter paper cone.
What will she see on the filter paper?

_____   1 mark

(d) What will she see in the beaker?

_____   1 mark

2 It is possible to separate salt from a solution of salt in water.

Describe how you could do this.
Mention the equipment you would use in your answer.

_____

_____   2 marks

3 Which two of these solids dissolve in water?

sugar ☐   tea leaves ☐   washing powder ☐

pepper ☐   chalk ☐   1 mark

4 Amy has a mixture of rice and flour.

Name a piece of equipment she could use to separate the rice from the flour.

_____   1 mark

TOTAL ☐

ROCKS AND SOILS

What you need to know

1 Describe and group rocks and soils according to their characteristics.

2 Understand the terms texture, hardness and permeability.

CHARACTERISTICS

- Rocks and soils are natural materials.

- Some rocks are harder than others, for example granite and marble are very hard; sandstone is soft, but not as soft as chalk.

ROCKS

- **Permeable** rocks let water soak through them, for example, sandstone, chalk, limestone.

- **Impermeable** rocks do not let water soak through them, for example, marble, flint, slate.

- Like other materials, different types of rock are used for different jobs, depending on their properties.

Marble is used for floors because it is very hard and can withstand a lot of wear.
Slate is used for roofs because it is impermeable and will therefore keep the rain out.

SOILS

- Soils are made of tiny bits of rock, dead plants and animals, air and water.

- Soil can have different **textures** and some soils allow water to drain through them more easily than others.

Sandy soil is quite dry and has lots of small air gaps.
Water drains through these gaps quite quickly.
Gravelly soil contains lots of small stones and pebbles.
It has larger air gaps which allow water to drain through quickly.
Clay soil is heavy and sticky. It doesn't have many air gaps so very little water can drain through it.

- Almost all plants need soil to grow in, but different plants prefer different types of soil.

ROCKS AND SOILS

1 Some children have been investigating rocks. They have put their information into a table.

Rocks	Scratched by: fingernail	2p coin	steel nail	Lets water through
Granite	no	no	no	no
Sandstone	no	yes	yes	yes
Flint	no	no	no	no
Chalk	yes	yes	yes	yes

(a) Which rocks are permeable? _____ 2 marks

(b) Name one rock that is harder than sandstone. _____ 1 mark

2 Ahmed and Paul are examining different soils. They put each soil into a filter paper in a funnel and poured 400 cm³ of water on to each soil. They collected the water in beakers. The volume of water (in cm³) was measured every two minutes. Here are their results.

	volume of water collected (cm³)		
	2 minutes	4 minutes	6 minutes
Test soil A	100	220	350
Test soil B	70	150	250
Test soil C	0	60	130

Test A
the soil contains mostly small gravel

Test B
the soil contains mostly sand

Test C
the soil contains mostly clay

(a) How did Ahmed and Paul present their results?

as a table ☐   as a diagram ☐   as a bar chart ☐   as a record ☐   1 mark

(b) Which factor was changed in each test? _____ 1 mark

(c) Give **ONE** way in which Ahmed and Paul made sure their tests were fair.

_____ 1 mark

(d) Which soil allowed the least water to drain through it?

soil in Test A ☐   soil in Test B ☐   soil in Test C ☐   1 mark

(e) After 20 minutes the water collected from Test A had reached 370 cm³. Explain why all the water did not filter through the soil in Test A.

_____ 1 mark

TOTAL ☐

CONDUCTORS AND INSULATORS

What you need to know

1 Know that some materials are good thermal conductors and some materials are good thermal insulators.

2 Know that some materials are good electrical conductors and some materials are good electrical insulators.

3 Understand that heat travels from a warmer area to a colder one.

THERMAL CONDUCTORS AND INSULATORS

- Some materials let **heat** travel through them easily. These materials are called **thermal conductors**.

  Most metals are good thermal conductors, for example, aluminium, copper and steel.

- Other materials do not let heat travel through them as easily. These are called thermal insulators.

  Good **thermal insulators** include wood, plastic, wool and polystyrene.

ELECTRICAL CONDUCTORS AND INSULATORS

- Some materials let **electricity** flow through them easily. These materials are called **electrical conductors**.

  Metals are generally good conductors of electricity. This is why all electrical items have metal parts and wires.

- Other materials do not allow electricity to flow through them. These materials are called **electrical insulators**.

  Most non-metals are good electrical insulators, for example, plastic, glass and rubber.

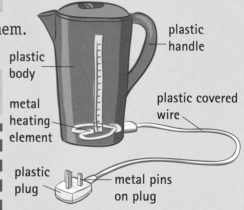

plastic handle

plastic body

metal heating element

plastic covered wire

plastic plug

metal pins on plug

> **SAFETY**
> It is important not to touch the metal parts of electrical items where electricity flows through as this is very dangerous. That is why switches, plugs and the other parts of electrical items that we need to touch are usually made of plastic.

TRAVELLING HEAT

- Heat travels from a warmer area to a cooler one which is why many winter clothes are made of wool (a thermal insulator) to help stop the heat from your body escaping into the cold air.
- Some pans have wooden or plastic handles to prevent the heat from the metal pan travelling through the handle and making it too hot to pick up.

CONDUCTORS AND INSULATORS

1 A material which allows heat to travel through it is called a thermal conductor.
A material which does not allow heat to travel through it is called a thermal insulator.

(a) Decide which of the following are conductors and which are insulators, and write their names in the table below.

plastic ruler
copper pipe
oven gloves
polystyrene tile
wooden spoon
cooking foil

thermal conductors	thermal insulators

3 marks

(b) Why is a saucepan made of metal, yet the handle is often made of wood or plastic?

____

1 mark

2 Steven has been investigating which materials are the best conductors of electricity. He has tested each material by making it part of an electrical circuit.

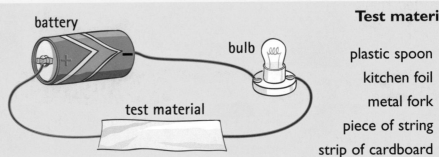

Test materials:

plastic spoon ☐
kitchen foil ☐
metal fork ☐
piece of string ☐
strip of cardboard ☐

(a) Decide whether the bulb will light up when each of the test materials in turn is placed in the circuit.
Tick the boxes in the diagram above for those that conduct electricity.

2 marks

(b) Steven notices that the wires he used in his circuit have strands of copper on the inside and plastic on the outside.
Explain why these two different materials are used.

(i) copper strands ____

____

1 mark

(ii) plastic coating ____

____

1 mark

TOTAL ☐

How did you score?

4 or less – try again!
5 or 6 – nearly there!
7 or 8 – well done!

SOIL INVESTIGATION

Typical garden soil is mostly made up of organic matter (from dead plants and animals) and usually contains grit and stones of different sizes.

Investigate a sample of soil taken from where you live.

You will need
rubber gloves
a cup or yogurt pot
a sheet of newspaper
2 bowls or jugs
a spoon
a colander or garden soil sieve
a kitchen sieve
filter paper or a double sheet of thick kitchen paper

What to do
Preferably use old cups, jugs, etc. that are no longer used for food, otherwise make sure you wash all the equipment thoroughly at the end of the investigation.

1 Why is this important?

_____

_____

_____

2 Start by scooping some soil into a cup or yogurt pot.
Wear rubber gloves to do this.
Why do you think it is sensible to wear rubber gloves?

_____

_____

3 Spread the soil you have collected on a sheet of newspaper.
Describe the texture and appearance of the soil.

_____

_____

_____

Now turn over for more investigation questions.

4 Now mix the soil well with about 500 ml of water in one of the bowls or jugs.

5 Pour the mixture through the colander or garden sieve, collecting the mixture that runs through in the second bowl (or jug).
Describe what you see in the colander and in the bowl.

_____

_____

_____

_____

6 Now pour the mixture through the kitchen sieve, collecting the mixture that runs through in the first bowl (or jug).
Describe what you see in the sieve and in the bowl.

_____

_____

_____

_____

7 Remove what was left in the sieve and place the filter paper or kitchen paper in the sieve. Finally pour the mixture through the filter/kitchen paper into the second bowl (or jug).
Describe what you see on the paper and in the bowl.

_____

_____

_____

8 You should now have separated most of the soil from the water.
Why do you think the water is not completely clear?

_____

_____

_____

Now that you have completed all the sections of this book, test your knowledge of scientific facts before you try the practice test.
Try to answer each question without looking back through the book first. If you're stuck then take a peek!

1   Name one life process which all living things can do.

2   Which word describes a material which does not let any light through?

3   Name the type of tooth which is used to grind and chew food.

4   Name one way in which seeds are dispersed.

5   How many months does it take for a human baby to grow inside its mother?

6   Which force makes objects fall towards the earth?

7   What is the main difference between vertebrates and invertebrates?

8   Give one way you could make a bulb brighter in a circuit.

9   In which part of the flower is pollen produced?

10 Is plastic a good electrical conductor or insulator?

11 What type of living things are producers?

12 At which time of day are shadows at their shortest?

13 Give one way in which a fish is adapted for life in water.

14 How long does it take the moon to orbit the earth?

15 Viruses and bacteria are which type of living thing?

_____

16 Melted chocolate can be cooled to form a solid again. What type of change is this an example of?

_____

17 Which force makes a feather fall to the ground more slowly than a stone?

_____

18 How can you separate salt from a solution of salt in water?

_____

19 Which bone protects the brain?

_____

20 Name a magnetic material.

_____

21 What should you do to make a recorder make a louder sound?

_____

22 Why is a switch used in a circuit?

_____

23 Which force is acting between the tyres and the road when the brakes are used?

_____

24 What is pulse rate a measure of?

_____

25 Which piece of equipment would you use to separate a mixture of small stones and sand?

_____

26 Which instrument makes notes which have a higher pitch: a violin or a double bass?

_____

27 Which part of the plant anchors it in the soil?

_____

28 What is the change from gas to liquid called?

_____   TOTAL

How did you score?

9 or less – try again!
10 to 20 – nearly there!
20 to 28 – well done!

SCIENCE KS2 PRACTICE TEST

1 **GROWING SWEET PEA PLANTS**

(a) Kyle is growing some sweet pea plants.

> Why do the petals have a strong perfume and bright colours?

_____

_____

1 mark

(b) Which part of the plant produces its food?

_____

1 mark

(c) The seeds in a sweet pea form in pods. When the seeds are ready to be dispersed the pods explode to release the seeds.

> Give **ONE** other way in which plants disperse their seeds.

_____

1 mark

(d) Kyle notices that the leaves on his plants are drooping and very dry.

> What does this tell you about the conditions in which the plants have been growing?

_____

_____

1 mark

(e) Kyle knows that the sweet pea plants are growing in a soil which is mostly clay. When he waters the plants he notices that the water does not soak through the soil but collects on the surface.

> Why does this happen?

_____

_____

1 mark

2 THE EARTH AND OTHER PLANETS

(a) Complete the labels to show the positions of the earth, sun and moon.

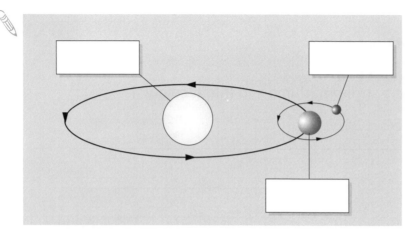

1 mark

The earth is 150 million kilometres from the sun.
It takes the earth 365 days to orbit the sun.

The earth is one of nine planets which orbit the sun.
Here are some facts about four of the other planets.

Planet	Distance from the sun (millions of kilometres)	Time taken to orbit the sun (days)
Mercury	58	88
Mars	228	687
Jupiter	778	4 329
Saturn	1 427	10 753

(b) Which of the four planets is furthest from the sun?

_____

1 mark

(c) How long does it take Jupiter to travel around the sun?

_____

1 mark

(d) What do the facts in the table tell you about the distance of a planet from the sun and the time it takes for that planet to orbit the sun?

_____

_____

1 mark

3 **HEDGEHOGS**

(a) Hedgehogs and slugs are both found in town gardens. The hedgehog feeds on insects, worms and slugs. Slugs eat vegetable crops, such as lettuce and cabbage.

> Write a food chain linking the slug, hedgehog and lettuce.

	→		→	

1 mark

(b) Slugs are treated as a pest in many gardens. Many are killed using chemicals.

> How might this affect the food chain?

_____

_____

1 mark

(c) The hedgehog can roll itself up into a ball when disturbed or attacked.

> What other feature does a hedgehog have which helps to protect it?

_____

1 mark

(d) The hedgehog lives and hunts for its food in dry leaves and in the bottom of hedges.

> Which feature makes it suited to this habitat?

_____

1 mark

4 PARACHUTES

(a) Liam is making parachutes from pieces of plastic cut from a carrier bag.
He cuts out a square of plastic and ties threads to each corner.
He then attaches the parachute to a ball of clay.

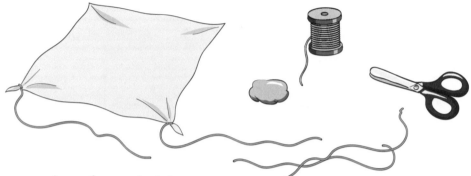

He drops the parachute from a height.
The forces of air resistance and gravity are acting
on the parachute.

Draw arrows on the diagram
to show these forces.

1 mark

(b) Liam makes three parachutes.
Here are the pieces of plastic he used for each one.

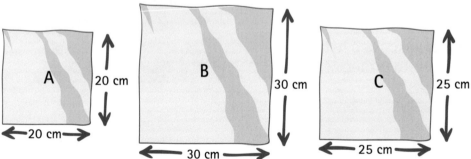

A   20 cm
←20 cm→

B   30 cm
← 30 cm →

C   25 cm
← 25 cm →

Which piece of plastic made the parachute fall fastest?

1 mark

(c) Name one factor which Liam must keep the same for each
parachute test to make sure he has carried out his tests fairly.

_____

1 mark

5 HEALTHY LIFESTYLE

(a) What is the main function of the heart in the human body?

✎ _____

1 mark

(b) Tania is cycling on an exercise bike. Her heart rate is being measured using a special electronic machine whilst she is cycling.
Below is the graph plotted on the screen of the machine.
Look at the way the graph changes between A and B.

What do you think she was doing at this time?

✎ _____

1 mark

(c) Tania knows that exercise is an important part of a healthy lifestyle.
She also knows that a balanced diet is important too.

What is meant by a balanced diet?

✎ _____

_____

1 mark

(d) Tania thinks that all drugs are harmful to the body?

Is she correct?

Circle   **Yes**   or   **No**

Explain your answer.

✎ _____

_____

1 mark

6 ELECTRIC CIRCUITS

(a) The amount of electricity flowing in a circuit is measured in amps.
Olivia is investigating how the amount of electricity flowing in a circuit changes with the number of batteries used. She is using a special meter to measure the amount of electricity flowing through the circuit.

Here are her readings:

No. of batteries	Meter reading (amps)
0	0
1	0·3
2	0·5
3	0·7

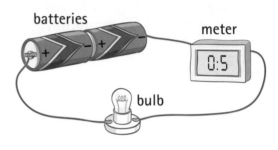

How does the number of batteries used change the amount of electricity flowing in the circuit?

_____

1 mark

(b) What happens to the bulb as Olivia adds each battery?

_____

1 mark

(c) Olivia changes her circuit to leave two batteries and the bulb.

Use these symbols to draw a diagram of her circuit.

battery   bulb

1 mark

(d) Olivia is using plastic-coated wires in her circuit.

Why are the wires coated with plastic?

_____

1 mark

7 SEPARATING A MIXTURE

(a) You have been given a mixture of iron filings, sand and salt in water.
You need to separate this mixture to get back the three different solids.
You are allowed to use the following equipment.

> Plan how you could separate the three different solids.

Write your plan here. Use diagrams to help explain what you would do.

3 marks

(b) > What safety measures should you take when doing your experiment?

1 mark

8 THERMAL INSULATION

(a) The temperature of a classroom is 19°C. Two beakers are filled with equal amounts of water at a temperature of 80°C. One beaker is wrapped in cotton wool. The temperature of the water in each beaker is measured every five minutes.

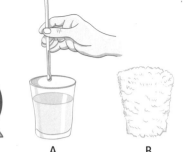

A   B

Here are the results.

	Temperature of water (°C)			
	0 minutes	5 minutes	10 minutes	15 minutes
beaker A	80	54	37	24
beaker B	80	72	65	59

Which piece of measuring equipment would be used to measure the temperature of the water?

_____

1 mark

(b) Which beaker of water cools more quickly?

beaker A ☐   beaker B ☐   both the same ☐

1 mark

(c) Why might it have cooled more quickly?

_____

_____

1 mark

(d) What do you think the temperature of the water in beaker A might be after 2 hours?

_____

1 mark

(e) Which two factors have been kept the same during the two tests?

(i) _____

(ii) _____

2 marks

92

9 **CASTIN** _Jules_

(a) Ni ght and shadows.
H to the ground.

> Draw an in the diagram
> to show how Nig see the stick.

(b) He notices that the stick casts
a shadow when the sun is shining.

> Why does the stick form a shadow?

[ ] *1 mark*

_____

_____

[ ] *1 mark*

(c) He measured the length of
the shadow every hour from
9:00 a.m. until 2:00 p.m.
Here are his results.

Length of shadow (cm)					
9:00 a.m.	10:00 a.m.	11:00 a.m.	12 noon	1:00 p.m.	2:00 p.m.
38	28	19	14	18	27

> Use Nigel's results
> to complete the
> line graph.

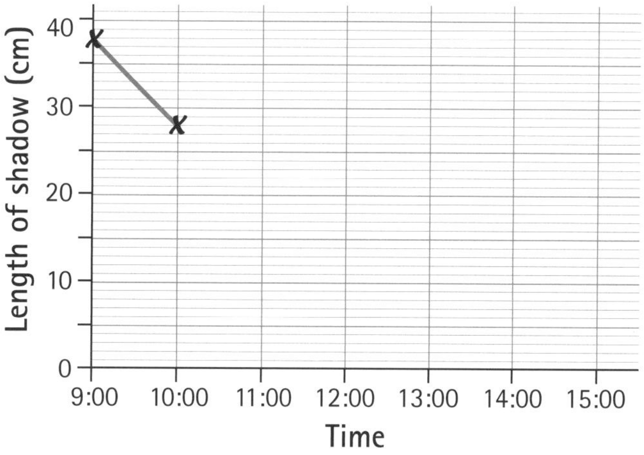

[Line graph: Length of shadow (cm) on y-axis from 0 to 40, Time on x-axis from 9:00 to 15:00. Two points plotted with X marks at (9:00, 38) and (10:00, 28) connected by a line.]

[ ] *2 marks*

(d) > What length would you expect the shadow to be at 3:00 p.m.?

[ ] *1 mark*

_____

(e) > Why does the length of the shadow change during the day?

[ ] *1 mark*

_____

_____

Total possible marks 40   SCORE [   ]

ANSWERS TO ACTIVITIES FOR WEEKS 1-8

Week 1 Monday
1 (a) E (b) J (c) A
2(a) To find out how the temperature of the water affects the time taken for the sugar to dissolve. To find out if warmer water makes sugar dissolve more quickly. (b) Tick 'The temperature of the water.' (c) Yes, because stirring makes the sugar dissolve more quickly. It would not make it a fair test.
(d) Glass beakers can easily break and shatter if not used with care. Water could be spilled making surfaces slippery.
Award marks for other sensible suggestions relating to the experiment e.g. 'He is using water which could be hot and he could be scalded'.

Week 1 Tuesday
1(a)

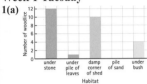

(b) To check that her first results were correct by seeing if the same thing happens again. (c) Woodlice prefer dark, damp habitats.
2(a) Tick 'graph'.
(b)

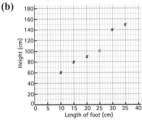

(c) Tick 'Taller people have larger feet.'

Week 1 Wednesday
1(a) Tick 'sun', 'lighted candle' and 'switched-on TV set'.
(b) Transparent - clear glass bottle; translucent - coloured tissue paper, pair of nylon tights; opaque - piece of wood.
Award 1 mark for three correct answers, 2 marks for all four correct.
(c)

Award 1 mark for correct lines and 1 mark for correct direction of arrows.
(d) To protect his eyes from very bright sunlight outside.

Week 1 Thursday
1(a) *Award the mark for an answer which explains that it is the earth that is moving not the sun.* (b) (i) The shadow gets shorter towards midday (lunchtime), then starts to get longer during the afternoon. (ii) noon
(c)

2 Tick 'comb' and 'wooden ruler'.
3(i) The shadow should start at the foot of the door - there should not be a gap.
(ii) The window would not cast a shadow.

Week 1 Friday
2 The investigation should show that the closer the object is to the light source, the larger the shadow.
3 The closer the shadow is to the light source, the 'fuzzier' or less sharp the edges of the shadow.

Week 2 Monday
1 Tick 'The earth orbits the sun.'
2 Tick 'gravity'.
3 Tick 'sphere'.
4(a) The light comes from the sun. (b) You cannot always see the side of the moon on which the sun is shining because the moon is in a different position each day as it is orbiting the earth.
Award 1 mark for a partial explanation.
(c) It could be cloudy.
5 Tick '28 days'.

Week 2 Tuesday
1(a) F, D (b) Hit the bottle harder.
2(a) Tick 'Quieter than when it was first hit.' (b) Tick 'silent'.
(c) He stopped the cymbal from vibrating and, as sound is caused by vibration, the sound stopped.
(d) Because sound does not travel well through the earplugs.
3 To protect his ears from damage caused by very loud sounds.

Week 2 Wednesday
1(a) The buzzer will not work because the switch is open.
(b)

(c) Add another battery.
(d) (i) The bulb will light up. (ii) The bulb will get hot.
2(a) *Two devices are needed for the mark, e.g. cooker, fridge, computer, TV.*
(b) The alarm clock may include a battery as an extra source of electricity.

Week 2 Thursday
1 Tick: iron nail, steel paperclip; Cross: wooden peg (given), aluminium foil, plastic spoon.
Award 1 mark for three correct answers and 2 for all four correct.
2 attract repel.
3(a) Tick 'To compare the strength of different magnets.' (b) 9
(c) Magnet D
4 The magnet will make sure that the door stays fully closed.

Week 2 Friday
1 The experiment should be repeated for each material to ensure that the results obtained are typical and that there are no mistakes.
2 Generally the greater the number of pins picked up, the stronger the magnet.
3 Covering with different materials will affect the number of pins picked up.
4 The experiment should show that a magnet will work under water.

Week 3 Monday
1 tug of war   ← →
  on hands of people pushing   → ←
  boat ↓
       ↑
2 Forces are balanced while the ball is on the ground. The foot exerts a force which unbalances the ball making it travel upwards.
3(a) The balloon will start to rise into the air.
(b) Show the forces: gravity   ↑
                                 upthrust   ↑
The upthrust arrow should be larger than the gravity arrow and in the opposite direction.
(c) Upthrust - whilst the balloon is in the air, its weight cannot be increased so the upthrust must be decreased.

Week 3 Tuesday
1 Gravity
2(a) pineapple (b) video tape (c) For the other objects the number of Newtons is double (different to) the number of cm. For the video they are both the same number. (d) He should repeat the experiment to compare his results.
(e) The larger the force, the longer the length of the spring. (f) 2 cm
3 The string should be drawn vertically (straight up and down) and not at an angle because gravity is pulling it towards the ground.

Week 3 Wednesday
1(a) The downward pull of the earth's gravity on the object. (b) 15 N
(c) The length of the spring is shorter. (d) The upthrust of the water on the stone cancels out some of the weight caused by gravity.
2(a) Show the forces: gravity   ↓
                                  upthrust   ↑
The arrows must be the same size in opposite directions.
(b) The force due to gravity is larger than the upthrust.

Week 3 Thursday
1(a) Tick 'air resistance'. (b) To make him go faster. (c) Tick 'friction'.
(d) It will make the force larger.
2(a) It will only take a few seconds for the object to fall and this clock cannot measure seconds. (b) Tick the box 'They will all take the same time.'
(c) The objects with a larger surface take longer to fall.

Week 3 Friday
1 The longer the band is pulled back (the more it is stretched), the further forward the piece of card will be catapulted.

2 The longer the band is stretched, the greater the force given to the piece of card.
3 Generally, the greater the force on an object, the further it will travel.
5 The surface could affect the distance travelled - a smooth surface could allow the piece of card to slide further when it lands.

Week 4 Monday
1 Tick grow , feed and reproduce .
2 Tick grass , cat and mushroom .
3(a) The plant turns its leaves and flowers towards the light.
(b) Reproduction

Week 4 Tuesday
1(a) A is an ant; B is a salamander. **(b)** bluebottle
2(a) A is a rose; B is a dandelion. **(b)** no
3 frog - amphibians; polar bear and dolphin - mammals; penguin and owl - birds; grass snake - reptiles; shark - fish
Award 1 mark for four or more correct answers, 2 marks for all correct.

Week 4 Wednesday
1
produces pollen
produces the fruit
supports the flower

2 So that the bee carries the pollen to another flower to pollinate it.
3(a) To make sure that he was testing the preferred colour only and not the preferred type of flower. **(b)** Yellow **(c)** He should make sure he records his results over 30 minutes as before. **(d)** No, this is unlikely, but he would expect similar numbers next time.

Week 4 Thursday
1(a) Roots **(b)** They would be thin, yellow and straggly.
(c) To investigate the effect of light on how seedlings grow.
(d) Light and temperature **(e)** Tape measure **(f)** Week 4 s measurement is incorrect. **(g)** A height in the range 150 cm to 160 cm.

Week 4 Friday
1 In this investigation plant A should grow best. Plant B should start to die as it dries up. Plant C should keep growing but start to grow spindly and its leaves start to lose their green colour.
2 Ways of ensuring a fair test include: using the same type of plants, using the same soil, using the same sized pots, watering the plants at the same time, giving each plant the same amount of water.
3 Light and sufficient water are needed for good plant growth.

Week 5 Monday
1 Tick woodlouse , red admiral butterfly , slug and daisy .
Award 1 mark for three correct answers and 2 marks for all four correct.
2 Lays eggs in water; has webbed feet.
3 Very strong, long root; produces hundreds of seeds which are easily dispersed by the wind.
4 Use the cardboard tray, cover with soil, spray with water and cover with black card.
Award 1 mark for selecting dark materials rather than clear plastic tray and cling film. Award second mark for selecting soil or sand which is then sprayed with water.

Week 5 Tuesday
1(a) Producers - algae, lettuce, grass; prey - rabbit, tadpole, fly; predator - spider, fox, blackbird.
Award 2 marks for all correct and 1 mark for five or six correct.
(b) algae → tadpole → blackbird; lettuce/grass → rabbit → fox
2(a) There would not be enough grass to feed the rabbits, voles and snails. Some would survive but there would be fewer for the owls, stoats and thrushes to prey on. *Award 1 mark for each of these main points.*
(b) The number of thrushes or field voles would fall as there would be more owls to prey on them. *Award 1 mark for each of these main points.*

Week 5 Wednesday
1(a) It contains too many fatty/sugary foods, there is no fruit and only potatoes (chips) for vegetables. **(b)** It contains foods from all the main food groups giving a balanced diet. **(c)** Tick It contains calcium for strong bones and teeth. **(d)** Possible answers are: take regular exercise, eat healthily, don t smoke, don t take drugs. **(e)** When you are driving a car you need to be able to make quick decisions and be careful. Alcohol makes people less able to do this. **(f)** No; drugs prescribed by doctors can cure diseases.

Week 5 Thursday
1(a) The speed at which the heart pumps blood around the body. **(b)** Tick table . **(c)** 115 beats per minute. **(d)** Because she has not done any activity which would make her pulse increase. **(e)** Her heart had to work harder to get oxygen to her muscles. **(f)** It has returned to her usual pulse rate when resting. **(g)** About 70 (also accept 71 or 72). **(h)** Multiply the number of beats by 6 to get the number of beats in 60 seconds (one minute).

Week 5 Friday
1 The experiment should be repeated to make sure that the pulse rate measured is correct and typical for each activity.
2 The length of time spent on each activity - 5 minutes.
3 After the activity is stopped the pulse rate begins to return to normal.
4 The investigation should show that the more vigorous the exercise the higher the pulse rate.
5 Four possible benefits of exercise are: it keeps the lungs healthy, increases muscle strength, makes bones stronger, helps reduce stress. There are other benefits.

Week 6 Monday
1(a) molar **(b)** Chewing or crushing or grinding food.
2(a) Tick an observation . **(b)** To get her into the habit of cleaning them properly every day.
3(a) This is when she brushed her teeth. **(b)** Possible answers are: visit the dentist regularly, floss them, use a mouthwash, eat fewer sugary foods, brush twice a day.

Week 6 Tuesday
1(a) fracture **(b)** Tick It keeps the bone in place. and It protects the bone from knocks. **(c)** Because he has not been able to use/exercise it fully.
2 Lines joining brain to skull, heart and lungs to rib cage and spinal cord to spine.
3 hip

Week 6 Wednesday
1(a) embryo, child, adult **(b)** adolescent **(c)** Tick 9 months . **(d)** They do not eat solid foods so do not need to bite or chew. **(e)** Possible answers could include: recognize different colours, recognize sounds, use hands to press buttons and turn knobs.

Week 6 Thursday
1(a) Tick a micro-organism .
2(a) A small amount **(b)** To see if the same thing happened to more than one barrel. **(c)** Tick microscope .
3 To make sure that the results were similar and accurate.
4 To stop the spread of the germs.
5(a) Mould would have started to grow on it or it could have gone stale/dried up. **(b)** He could have kept it in the freezer.

Week 6 Friday
1 The conclusion should make a statement about how many people in your family eat a healthy diet based on the number of portions of fruit and vegetables they eat.
2 Answers should recognize that the data was only collected for one day for a small number of people.

Week 7 Monday
1(a) Clear polythene and Perspex **(b)** It is not waterproof.
(c) Clear polythene; it is both waterproof and flexible.
2 reflective patches: so that she can be seen in the dark
rubber sole: to cushion the foot when it hits the ground
waterproof fabric: to keep the feet dry when it is raining

Week 7 Tuesday
1(a) solid, gas, liquid, (reading downwards).
(b) The gas in the liquid was able to escape into the air.
2(a) Tick thickness .
(b) The thicker the liquid, the longer it takes the marble to fall through it.
3(a) Helium is lighter than air. **(b)** The gas mixes with the air.

Week 7 Wednesday
1(a) Starting from top left, reading clockwise, the order is: B, A, C, D. *Award 1 mark for two correct and 2 marks for all four correct.* **(b)** Tick gas changes to liquid . **(c)** It can be changed back. **(d)** Examples could include: chocolate melting/setting, water freezing/thawing.
2(a) It will start to melt (thaw). **(b)** The soup is heating up/boiling.
(c) The water in the soup would evaporate and the rest would burn on the pan.

Week 7 Thursday
1(a) Tick none of them . (b) Non-reversible (or allow chemical).
(c) It would burn. (d) It melts. (e) It will turn it into a liquid which will make it easier to spread on the cake. (f) burn (g) Tick observation .
(h) It will have burned and turned into charcoal.

Week 7 Friday
Three places: a warm place could be above a radiator or in an airing cupboard. A cool place could be on a shaded windowsill or next to the front door. A cold place could be in the fridge or cellar.
1 Use saucers which are the same size containing the same amount of water and observe each of them at the same time each day.
2 The investigation should show that the warmer the place the quicker the water will evaporate.

Week 8 Monday
1(a) Stir it. (b) The salt will stop dissolving as more is added.
(c) The undissolved salt will be left on the filter paper. (d) The salt dissolved in the water (salt solution) will collect in the beaker.
2 Heat the solution in a beaker over a burner/in a pan on a cooking ring until all the water evaporates to leave the solid salt in the bottom.
3 Tick sugar and washing powder .
4 Sieve (strainer).

Week 8 Tuesday
1(a) Sandstone and chalk. (b) Granite or flint.
2(a) Tick table . (b) Type of soil. (c) They used the same amount of water for all three soils; they measured the water collected every 2 minutes for all three soils. (d) Tick soil in Test C . (e) Some of the water was absorbed by the soil.

Week 8 Wednesday
1(a) Thermal conductors: copper pipe, cooking foil.
Thermal insulators: oven gloves, wooden spoon, polystyrene tile, plastic ruler.
Award 1 mark for any two correct, 2 marks for any four correct and 3 marks for all six correct.
(b) The metal body conducts heat well to help cook the food. The wooden handle does not conduct heat making it safer to pick up.
2(a) Tick kitchen foil and metal fork . (b) (i) The copper strands are good conductors of electricity. (ii) The plastic coating is a good electrical insulator so that when you touch the wires you don t get a shock.

Week 8 Thursday
1 Soil contains bacteria which could be harmful so equipment should be cleaned thoroughly.
2 Rubber gloves should be worn for hygiene reasons and for safety as the soil may contain sharp stones or glass.
3 The soil should be described in terms of its colour, texture and content, for example, light brown, dry with bits of grit and small stones.
5-7 The different stages of separation should remove different-sized particles.
8 The water left will not be completely clear as some very fine particles of soil may be left in it.

Week 8 Friday
Science Quiz
1 reproduce, feed, grow
2 opaque
3 molar
4 wind, animal, explosion
5 9 months
6 gravity
7 vertebrates have a backbone, invertebrates do not
8 add another battery, shorten the wires
9 stamen
10 insulator
11 green plants
12 around midday (noon)
13 streamlined, has gills, has fins, lays eggs in water
14 28 days
15 micro-organisms
16 reversible
17 air resistance
18 evaporate water from the solid
19 skull
20 steel or iron
21 blow it harder
22 to break the flow of electricity
23 friction
24 the rate at which blood is pumped by the heart
25 sieve
26 violin
27 roots
28 condensation

PRACTICE TEST ANSWERS

1 Growing sweet pea plants
(a) To attract insects so that they can be pollinated. (b) leaves
(c) By the wind, in water, by animals (on fur, feet, droppings).
(d) The soil in which the plants are growing has been allowed to dry out, or the soil is very dry. (e) The particles of soil are tightly packed and do not allow water to pass through very easily.

2 The earth and other planets
(a) Reading clockwise from left: sun, moon, earth. (b) Saturn
(c) 4 329 days (d) The further away the planet is from the sun, the longer its orbit.

3 Hedgehogs
(a) lettuce → slug → hedgehog (b) Either it would reduce the number of slugs allowing more lettuces to grow, or, fewer slugs would mean less food for the hedgehogs. (c) spines (d) Long nose for burrowing/smelling, or, clawed feet for pulling at leaves/holding prey.

4 Parachutes
(a) Arrows as shown opposite (the downwards arrow must be larger than the upwards arrow)
(b) Shape A (smallest area) (c) Drop from the same height or keep the same ball of clay.

5 Healthy lifestyle
(a) It pumps blood around the body. (b) Cycling faster. (c) One which includes food from all food groups. (d) No, because some drugs prescribed by doctors help to cure diseases.

6 Electric circuits
(a) The higher the number of batteries, the greater the amount of electricity flowing through the circuit. (b) The bulb shines more brightly.
(c)

(d) Plastic is a good insulator and will prevent her from getting a shock or burn.

7 Separating a mixture
(a) First, pour the mixture through the filter paper to remove the sand and iron filings. Use the magnet to separate the iron filings from the sand. The salt which will have dissolved in the water runs through the filter and can then be heated on the camping stove until it evaporates leaving the salt in the pan.
Award 1 mark for using a magnet to remove the iron filings. Award 1 mark for using filter paper to leave a salt solution. Award 1 mark for evaporating the solution to leave salt.
(b) Use gloves or tongs to handle hot equipment, or use goggles to protect eyes from fine particles, boiling water.

8 Thermal insulation
(a) thermometer (b) beaker A (c) It is not insulated. (d) The temperature will drop to 19°C which is the temperature of the room. (e) The amount of water in each beaker; how often each temperature is taken.

9 Casting shadows
(a)

(b) The stick is opaque so light cannot pass through it so it casts a shadow.
(c)

(d) A length between 37 cm and 39 cm. (e) Shadows are longest when the sun is low in the sky and shortest when the sun is overhead.

Awarding a level for the practice test

There are 40 possible marks on the science practice test. Compare your child s final score with the figures in the table below and read off the corresponding level. The marks required for each level are approximately based on those used to determine levels in the KS2 National Tests where most pupils are expected to achieve Level 4.

Level	Score
N	8 or less
2	9-10
3	11-19
4	20-31
5	32-40